Servant to the Phoenix
by
Arthur E. Levick

Volume 1

Printed and published by:
ALD Design & Print
279 Sharrow Vale Road
Sheffield S11 8ZF

Telephone 0114 267 9402

© Arthur Levick 2011

E-mail a.lofthouse@btinternet.com

ISBN 9781901587913

First published September 2011

I would like to take this opportunity to dedicate this book to my wife Janet who put up with endless hours of tapping away on my word processor, to my cousin Kathleen Whittle who retyped all my work and to Tony Hunter for letting me use his memory when mine failed and to the South Yorkshire Fire and Rescue Service, for letting me use their photographs also the Sheffield Fire Museum photographs.

Also Edward Mullins, John Hague of N.A.R.F. website for the use of their photographs.

Two man Hook Ladder

Contents

Prologue

"Kerr--boom".

Glass showered down into the street, followed by further explosive reports, whilst smoke and flames escaped from the now shattered windows of the building. Meanwhile the Fire Chief looked anxiously towards the front opening where he had committed his fire crews.

Then out of this blazing hell staggered a single fireman, his legs giving way to exhaustion as he got to his Chief.

"We did it Sir", he gasped.

"Good, I knew I could rely on you," replied the Chief, pushing his helmet to the back of his head.

For a moment they were silent, as the Chief knelt cradling the exhausted fireman in his arms, and then he spoke once more.

"What happened to the Smiley Cockney, Rowbotham, Brown, Tommy Atkins?" queried the Chief.

"All dead, Sir."

"God, they were brave men."

"Yes Sir, but we saved the Budgie, and that got to make it worthwhile."

"True," replied the Chief, " but where is the bird."

"You're knelt on it, Sir."

We have all seen this type of film depiction of how firemen behave from 'When the Bell goes down' to 'Backdraft'. Yet this book is not about fictitious characters doing daring deeds, this is about real men who worked as a team, who had all the human weaknesses, nevertheless were prepared to put their life on the line in the service to the general public.

When I joined the Service in the 1960s it was known as the Fire Brigade. We were Firemen, who served the public when all others had failed; we were the last hope for many. Our trade had been learnt and honed to perfection during the blitz of this country's cities and towns, and the men of that period handed to their successors, an expertise of sound knowledge through battles fought on the fire ground. We were not hampered as now with Health and Safety, and it is hoped that those who followed us still manage to have pride and joy in the service as we did.

Aux Fm. 946 Levick

Volume 1

Chapter 1

The Recruit Years 1964 – 66

You may ask yourself what makes men enrol into an occupation where you go towards the danger, when all human reaction is to do the contrary.

I first witnessed in 1963 firemen in a new light. It was during those early March gales of that same year which ripped Sheffield apart. At that time I was working as an apprentice Constructional Plater/Welder. I could try and fill you with written diatribe of why I enrolled. Like wanting to serve the community, hero worship, the uniform, and the excitement, reliable employment. Maybe it was some part of all those but one thing is for certain it wasn't being overpaid.

I first tried out what the job entailed by joining the Auxiliary Fire Service (A.Fm.946), which was part of the Civil Defence Organisation of this country. After just nine months I thought I knew enough to alter my career choice to that of a full time fireman. What I didn't expect when I joined the Sheffield Fire Brigade was to be cast into a time warp where men who had not served in the armed forces were placed in the role of a second-class citizen.

After our initial training of four weeks at Mansfield Road, Intake, my recruit's course of twelve men was transferred out to our first stations. It was deemed lucky for me and Roger Pearson an old school classmate, that we had been sent to Elm Lane, which was Station Officer Reaney's command, and I was thought even more fortunate to be on Tom Varleys shift that being Blue Watch.

During our induction weeks I had very little trouble apart from the fact that I take a ten-inch pace longer than anybody I know. So when I march, within a few steps I am ready for overtaking whoever is in front of me or if I lead off I found I marched alone. It would be fair to say marching was never my best activity. I also found the words of command a bit strange,
"Biff, Bight biff, bight, translated back into English meant left, right, left right. Wilt or Walt was halt, Squid Wilt meant, squad halt."
When I was three years old I was severely traumatized by a neighbour who

kicked a football direct into my face. The shock of this injury caused me to have an acute stammer, which took until I was twelve before it was corrected out. Now at nineteen we were being instructed with men who thought it sounded wonderful to have a speech impediment. The letter 'H' was either dropped off completely or added when not necessary. Typical drill commands from the instructor would sound like,

"Crews Number from the weft. Un, oo, free fourwer, fiva and so on. Translated back into English.

Crews number from the left, one, two, three, four, five.
Or Squid shun, crew Un, weel pitch the ladder to the dwrill tower, taking aloft Un line of hose terminating in a H-London bwranch, and weel have a Hittle more Heffort."

" Squad attention, Crew one, will pitch the ladder to the drill tower, taking aloft one line of hose terminating in a London Branch (nozzle), and we will have a little more effort. From what I gather this clipped tongued language was standard army banter used by all drill Sergeants: furthermore, if it was good enough for General Bernard Montgomery to speak like it then a bleedin' low life recruit better get use to it.

The induction course was to knock out the individual in you and to make you act as a team member. This was brought home to me very quickly when I took up my first posting. Tom Varley for several months had been asking when his shift was going to get its senior hand the Leading Fireman. Yet instead of getting a rank with a single chrome bar on his shoulders, he got a raw recruit.
"I don't need a recruit," he reprimanded Station Officer Albert Reaney, "I've already got Furniss, and Rosier still doing their probationary period, Parker, and Smith aren't much out of their recruits period, leaving me with Cappy Kendrick, Horseley and young Ash. You just got rid of Fox, now you are lumbering me with another recruit."

"Welcome to Elm Lane," I thought, as the two officers wrangled over why I had been sent.
"He is only here temporary Tom, soon as your Leading Fireman comes he'll be shipped out," said Stn.O. Reaney.

To Tom, I was about as useful as a chocolate fire guard, my knowledge on firemanship was zero, and therefore he put me into the Watchroom when ever he could, to give him the most experienced fire crew on the Bedford

Water Tender. The only time I was excused Watchroom duties was at drill times. The only plus side to this was it gave me good grounding in taking and receiving messages: also' it gave me the opportunity to study the Home Office manuals. I don't believe I wasted those moments, but to say I never had problems in taking calls would be down right lies.

'Happy' Wostenholme was a Control room operator, and under normal work pressures he was well on top of his job but occasionally something or someone would wind this man up and he would lose his cool and his voice octaves became that of a Choir boy. One incident sticks in my mind very clearly. I hadn't been at Elm lane very long when I received a call from 'Happy', to send our appliance to what sounded like, "Bus Meadows."

I took down all the details of this chimney fire and started to relay back the message for verification address of incident.

"No, not Bus Meadows," a pause and what sounded again like "Bus Meadows".
"Bus Meadows", I repeated.
"No, Bus MEADOWS," he squeaked.
"Bush Meadow," very nervous I questioned.
"No you stupid bastard, BUS MEADOWS," he squealed. Now one thing gets up my nose quickly is to be called a bastard.

In anger over what had been said to me, I lost control and I grabbed hold of the handset and shouted down the line, "Who are you calling a bastard, you little shit." All my calm had gone, the fire call was secondary in my mind, and moreover all I wanted to do was get my hands around his scrawny neck and wring the life out of him. Just then Jack Furniss came into the Watchroom and took the telephone from me.

"Calm down Happy, calm down," he pleaded. Picking up the message pad and he asked," "Is this call to Busk Meadows," queried Jack.
"That's what I have been saying to that idiot."

The appliance was dispatched and quiet fell upon the Watchroom. That was until Tom got back and he rollicked me, for loosing my temper. Now I wasn't the only one to suffer from this man. Jack also had his problems when taking calls from him.

In Furniss's case it was to Brightholme Lea Lane, yet when you are not sure of the address, squealing sounds take on a different air, to when you are calm.

To Jack it was possibly Brightside Lane, Bright Lane, Holme Lane, but Brightholme Lea Lane was not in Jack's vocabulary. He also suffered with Baccarosses Garage, which turned out to be Back of Ross's Garage. Bert Rosier was another to misinterpret his messages. Speaking with his Godmanchester, Cambridgeshire drawl. He asked Happy, " if he had said Gas Fire,"

"You say, Gas fire at Penn Fold Road,"
"No, Gas fire."
"I soy spell message for me," asked Bert
"G or Golf, R for Roger, A for Alpha, S for Sugar, S for Sugar," spelled Happy.
"That's Grarss, you silly Yorkshireman," chided Bert.

The appliance, with me aboard after I had proved myself in Tom's eyes fit enough to be of some use, slipped out of the station to the fire. As the engine pulled out through the door I heard Bert shout, " trouble with you Nartherners you don't speak Facking properly."

Although I never doubted my own ability, like I said it took several month before I started riding with any regularity to anything but the smallest of incidents, gaining my place in Tom's Team. My first house fire was to the Southey area of Sheffield to an old Brigadier and his Batman. Horseley and Ash had got the hose reel to work after Terry Smith had driven the appliance to the incident. My instruction from Station Officer Reaney was to stay close to Tom and be of assistance where I could. This I did helping and pulling the hose reel to the side main entrance. Just then Reaney shouted to Tom, "Ventilate."

"Right Lad, follow me," commanded Tom, "take a good intake of air and help me unfasten the widows." Stooping low he ducked under the smoke level and made his way toward the staircase. Checking I was still with him, he charged up the staircase until he reached the landing window and with a swift smack of his large fist, the catch was released and the window opened, where he took his second breath. My air had run out half way up the stairs and my eyes stung with the smoke.

"Take another gob full, lad," he ordered, "and follow me to the bedrooms."
I looked in wonderment at this asbestos lunged being, which breathed fire and air in equal measure. I was in a mind to tell him to carry on his own, for I was quite comfortable breathing in fresh air from the open landing window.

"Follow me."
Twice more we did the same enter a room and slid open the windows to let in fresh air. Outside the third bedroom he turned and pulled me through the thinning smoke.
"Right Lad, this is yours."

With caution I moved to the door wrapping my coat sleeve around my hand to stop any heat from the door handle burning it. With my other hand I checked for heat on its surface; none could be felt, so I pressed down the handle and turned away as I had been shown. No fire flash, just thick smoke billowed out of this small room.

"Undo the window, then check the bed and under it for bodies," Tom commanded.

This I did, but with the thick smoke stinging my eyes and my lungs bursting for fresh air, I was keen to be finished. When I felt something under the bed, a metal object, yet definitely not a Poe or pot, I bent down to inspect the object but the smoke was still too thick for my stinging eyes. Then I made a fatal mistake - I tugged at this metal object, which became suddenly free and urine together with human excrement sloshed towards my face.

Tom burst out laughing and started to make his way out back down the stairs. Still laughing he called back, "Come on lad, and remember we don't leave peoples property looking shitty." I rinsed myself down as much as I could with the water from the hose reel, when Tom and Albert came toward the back of the appliance.

"Do you think they were puffs," asked Albert Reaney.
"Don't know Sir, but Arthur has inspected their shit, ask him if any was countersunk" he quipped.

On returning to the station Tom gave me one or two tips about house fires, and I finally discovered why the Breathing Apparatus sheep skin neckband always looked so clean and white. The reason was very simple - they hardly ever used them. Smoke gobbling was the norm and you were expected to take punishment from fires without moaning.

As time passed I was slowly inducted into the team that was Blue Watch. Yet no matter what I did I could never be classed as equal to an ex-serviceman. This niggled me a lot, for whilst in the steelworks I was in charge of not only seeing that jobs got out on time but also created a profit for the company I worked for. In addition I had the responsibility to see that structures I made wouldn't collapse. (At this present time 1998 I can still take you to bridges and other constructions that I helped to make, and if they are maintained they will still be here in another hundred years.)

Yet when good jobs were handed out the recruit always got the worst of the deal that was the way they had been educated and that was the way I was to be treated. The army stories of the firemen often amused me at meal times Dick Ash told of how he on being 'Called up', was asked could he ride a bike. So he told them he could, only to find out that the drill Sergeant had meant could he ride a motorbike. On being given a 500cc motorbike he tried to explain there had been a misunderstanding but the army like the fire service make a decision and never reverse it, unless absolutely forced.

"Wight you lot, start up your bikes, select first gear and go in a single file around the perimeter of the parade ground," shouted the Sergeant. One by one the bikes were kick-started and rode off, that was until it came to Dick's turn.

"Starting wasn't a problem," said Dick, "yet when I selected the first gear and let out the clutch. I must have revved a little too much, because the bike roared forward a great rate of knots toward one of the Nissen huts, which suddenly jumped out, to stop my velocipedes accelerated motion (I crashed).   Laying dazed on the floor with the bike partly on my legs I became aware that the Sergeant was standing over me."

" Who gave you bleedin' permission to dismount? Get from under that wreck and go get another bike," barked the Sergeant.

Bert told of his early days as Guardsman at Pirbright when being inspected by the Sergeant who walked along the ranks until he stood in front of him.
"Ello, ello. What have we here, are you a G-nomee, or are you stood in a hole," he shouted, referring to Bert's vertical deficiency than others on parade. I don't know why some of these stories stuck with me perhaps it was their way of saying "Don't worry, we have all been through the mill."

Tom had made 'Cappy Kendrick' my mentor and at first I resented his guidance but over the months, and eventually over the years I knew him, I would rely on his good judgment. Albert Reaney used to say there is fireman clean, and then there is Kendrick and Wardle clean. In due time my name would be added to this list. Yet for all the time I spent on station waiting for my turn to go Leeds Central Training School at Gipton, nothing could have prepared me for those next twelve weeks of hell.

Personally I am a home lover and my family has always been very dear to my heart. It was unfortunate that my Grandmother died whilst I was at Gipton and her death saddens me beyond any grief up to that time. The lack of respect the instructors had for you and a regime where those who were named on the first day for demonstration purposes, was a recipe for legalized bullying. Not that any of them would dream of trying physical harm whilst out of uniform, they applied the Fire Service discipline code to the letter. Using its text to hide their latent cowardice.

None more than a little man called 'Chalky' White; although not my instructor he often had the squads on parade for inspection. This little excuse of a man would take delight in goading you, and I was informed by Doug Binnington a colleague who also suffered of being named man. That in our billet Mick Curtis was running a book as to whether I would flatten that little creep. Fortunately for me I had started courting Janet Rawson, and I didn't want her to think that I couldn't hold a job down as we intended to get married one day. It was conversation one leave weekend that Janet said, " to complete the course and if I passed then the system wouldn't have beat me and I could still leave at anytime with my head held high."

My own squad leader was Welsh/Leeds Sub officer called Davies, and it was he who took me nearly to my breaking point. We used to do the fireman's lift /carry downs drill regular at some part of the day, usually as patient and one carry down. Although I never minded carrying downs it was Brian Fletcher who pointed towards me, when Davies asked who was to do the last carry of the afternoon.

"Right Fletcher, you go down, Levick can carry me."

I whispered a few adjectives to Brian for missing his turn and watched him start his descent, and moved over to Davies to lift him onto my shoulders. On gaining the ladder I settled Davies into a comfortable carry position for me. Left hand, left foot we started our descent, then it struck me this man who I was carrying, for ten-week had been on my back metaphorically all that time.

"What would you do if I slipped," I asked.

Suddenly his hands grabbed my drill belt, and I knew worry had entered his head.

"I think I could hold onto the rounds of the ladder longer than you could my belt," I said.

"Are you having difficulty," he quietly inquired, but a doubt was getting stronger in his head.

I moved my body further out from the ladder making it more difficult for him to grab hold should I decide to throw him off.

"One good hitch, and I reckon you'd be off my back for good," I replied.

"Levick, take me down," he said, his finger knuckles holding my belt by now were white.

I re-arranged him on my back, juggling him across my shoulders until his testicles were on my shoulder where they would cause him the most discomfort. Then humming the Edith Piaf song 'No Regrets', I started back down and getting to the bottom I gently lowered him safely to the ground.

I expected to be put on another charge to accompany the one when I told the cook what she could do when she scalded my hands, but he said nothing, only a doubt as to whether or not I would have carried my threat out. My name from then on all but disappeared from his lips, which suited us both. To give him credit though he was the best teacher of hook ladders and whilst others trembled their way to the top of the drill tower, we had mastered it in the first lesson, and it was our squad who were filmed for the Kingston upon Hull Training film. The time spent at Leeds was not for me the best, and I was glad to be back, with the lads at Elm Lane.

Several incidents whilst doing my probationary period raised me in stature a little with my peers. The first was when Sheffield had its second hurricane force gale in two years; the damaged caused was exacerbated by damage the previous year. For weeks we climbed and cut loose fitting from rooftops, and by the end of this emergency period I think I could say that I had achieved the agility of those I had admired in 1963. With my increased training and fire ground knowledge I had become a lesser burden for Tom and Blue Watch. Furthermore Tom had four young men who were equal to one another with their firemanship, adding to that I discovered I had passed my Leading Fireman's examination which took me up and equal in knowledge to my senior colleagues, which also reflected well on Watch Officers. The etiquette mistakes I had made when I first joined had been smoothed out. Yet it still brings a smile to recall the day not long after being posted to Elm Lane. Jack had told me that if the Chief should come or any senior officer the Control Room Officer at Division Street would give me warning. This gave you or the officer in charge of the station, from being caught with your pants down. If such an officer did come, he would always report direct to you on Watchroom duty so that the Central Manning knew where they were, in case of emergencies. So it was inevitable that not long after this conversation a black Humber saloon car drove passed my window with what appeared to be a senior officer at the driving wheel. I looked at my telephone console and no white bull's eyes tallies had dropped to warn me, that someone was trying to get in contact with me, and from my limited view from the Watchroom, the driver had gone elsewhere. Perhaps I had been mistaken, so I sat down once again to read my manuals, only this time to catch sight of Assistant Chief Fire Officer Lambert coming from the gardens.

"The bastards," I thought, "them down at H.Q. had set me up."

So once again I rose from my seat and was ready to place my cap upon my head ready to salute the ACO, on his entrance. Three times he moved to the door only to stop and inspect something or other that caught his eye. Three times I braced myself to give him the full salutation.

"Fireman Levick on Watchroom duty.
Station Officer Reaney Officer in charge.
Water Tender available."

By the time of his fourth stop I was fed up of this cat and mouse waiting so I resumed my studies until he decided to call in to see me. A short while later the handle of the Watchroom door turned and the door slightly cracked open and Mr. Lambert's head poked through the gap created. He looked at me, and I returned the gaze. I rose to my feet and started to place my cap on my head once again. Now in the steelworks bosses were not slightly interested in correct social greetings, only in you being respectful and doing your job well enough for them to make money out of your labour. Fire brigade was a different matter; it was all pomp and ceremony. For a few seconds we stood staring at each other before I spoke.

"Are you coming in, if so I'll give you the salutation? If not please shut the door as you leave."

With that he quietly shut the door and walked away back to Station Officer's office; I in turn informed control that Lambert was on my station and I returned to my seat and studies. Suddenly all hell broke loose. Telephone Bull's- Eyes on the switchboard panel were dropping by the microsecond, and

11

Blue watch Arthur, John, Tom, Jack Furniss, & Terry Smithy

Ajax ladder practice Elm Lane

into this confusion then strode Tom.

"What the hell have you said lad," he enquired.

"Nothing," I replied, still trying to reason what had so upset Lambert.

Keith Parker was put into the Watchroom to take over my duties, whilst Tom and I did a quick march over to the office. Now under normal circumstances for Albert to want to speak to me it would have needed a fortnight's planning before such a meeting was convenient to him to see me, but today was different; today I was honoured by an immediate appointment.

Tom knocked on the door and was summoned in, only to return in a fraction later to bring me before my ACFO and my Station Officer. Reaney's neck was crimson in colour and his lips and teeth were tightly shut. As he spoke there was an air of a ventriloquist who was trying to gain his composure, but failing miserably.

"You know who this officer is?" he asked, jerking his head forward. The moment didn't seem right for a Smart Alec answer, so I looked at Lambert and said, "It's the A.C.F.O., sir."

"Correct, Fm. Levick. And can you tell me why, according to you, he now doesn't merit the salutation?" His chin extended on finishing his speech.

I turned and faced Lambert. "Because you didn't come into the Watchroom like you are supposed to do," I replied. Lambert smiled, "He is right Mr Reaney, I didn't go in, but if it's all the same to you lad, I'd like it in the future." This was not the time to argue about following his own commands, so I looked back to the Station Officer. Everything had calmed down now; the natural colour was flowing back into Reaney' face and neck. Varley's regimented pose eased as the tension left the room; I only wished I would be allowed to follow it. The Lambert incident started the reputation of me being a straight talker or as Tom said to Lambert. " He's a bit of a rough diamond."

Mind you if I slipped up by doing or saying the wrong thing so could Albert Reaney. Station Officer Reaney was a lovely man to witness and work under. Like all eccentrics he loved playing to an audience and none gave him a better stage than when we were called out on an emergency call. If held up by traffic whilst proceeding to an incident he would lean out of the appliance side window and wave the 'call out sheet' at the offending motorists. Whilst stabbing it vigorously would shout, "this is not shopping list we going to collect, or can't you hear these warning bells what do you think this is a ruddy ice cream van."

In Reaney's eyes he wanted the general public to know he was in charge and to cross him was tantamount to blasphemy. So when at a house fire, where shortly before the married female occupant was entertaining her soldier lover, he attempted to stop the amour leaving the scene before his investigation was complete. It was a battle of wills, the brute strength of the soldier and Reaney's charisma.

"It's a silly point," he began as usual, "but you may have been cause of this fire. Therefore I request that you stay, until I have fully ascertained the cause of this fire."
"F--- you mate, I can't stop around for you."
"Well I have the power to make you stay for as long as I require," responded Albert.

"Look ol' man, believe me you aint stopping me going," snapped the soldier.
"Then my men will make you stay," gestured Reaney making a sweeping hand gesture in Jack's and my direction.

Now I have never been averse to fighting but it isn't what I expected being a fireman was about. That, plus having tangled with soldiers in pub skirmishes, the prospect of have having my wedding tackle crushed by a studded boot before they had been properly worn in didn't appeal to me.

Fortunately for me and I'll say Jack, that Varley had had the true situation explained to him by the woman and he smoothed the way for the soldier to make a discreet exit. Another incident with Reaney I'll never forget was on a Wade Street. It was to a small house fire, which had been quickly extinguished by us on arrival. Several house occupants had suffered burns whilst they had tried to fight the fire until we arrived. After the initial hullabaloo Albert thrust a small three-year old child at me and I was instructed, "to see to him." With tears rolling down his face I tried to ask if he was hurt. A small arm was thrust in my direction.

On his fore arm was a deep swollen mauve-red mark about eight inches long. So immediately I got some cold water from the machine and cooled the affected area for some minutes before applying the best spiral bandaging you could ever wish to see. Taking the lad by now who was only whimpering toward an awaiting ambulance I was approached by the lad's mother.
"What's up we 'im"?
"He's got a slight burn to his forearm," I replied.
"No he bleedin' hasn't, that birth mark he all us 'ad."
Taking charge of the child once more they both walked towards the

ambulance

"I don't know what you are crying for," I heard the mother say.

"So shut up."

Thankfully for me no one else witnessed my mistake, only I had learned a valuable lesson birth marks and first-degree burns can look similar. So Check. The occasion that raised me and took me from the recruit status, to being regarded as a fireman worth his salt happened near to the end of my probationary period.

Tom Varley had been transferred to Division Street, and the Chief's son Barry Jones had taken up this vacant post. This was very convenient, to think that he had just transferred back from the West Riding Brigade, and out of the blue a post near to his home should become available. It has never failed to amaze me that when positions or job vacancies come about, those senior manager's or union official's kith and kin always appear on the list of successful applicants. Maybe I am just cynical; perhaps when a few months later Albert Reaney got his promotion, it was on merit alone, and not for convincing Tom to move out quietly. So when Reaney goes, our new Station Officer is to be Bill Sinclair.

Well whatever happened Barry was now our new Sub Officer and we had a Leading Fireman in the shape of Walt Dawes. To be honest, we had another for a short while before him 'Bud' Roberts. If Walt was to be my- making as a better fireman, Bud certainly raised a few smiles whilst he was here with his quips and endless joke telling.

One early spring morning, Barry had taken us for our drill session and had handed over to Walt to carry on our additional training. All the while we drilled, a young man sat on the wall watching our every move. This was nothing unusual during any morning of the spring and summer months for people to stop and watch our drill exhibitions. So no one took much notice of this man. When Barry came out from the office a short while later to replace his kit onto the machine the young man got up and went over to Barry.

"Sorry to bother you," he said, "but I'm working on the old people's flats and the one next to the one I'm re-pointing has got a heck of a chimney fire."

"Walt! Chimney fire," shouted Barry

Drill came to a halt immediately and we made up the gear we had taken from the Wr.T. There was a sense of urgency in the make-up, but not one of panic. Whilst this was happening Barry got the details from the workman and relayed them to Terry in the Watchroom, to dispatch to Control.

As we moved off, Barry told the young man to get aboard and he could guide us if needed. This wasn't necessary, for as we came around the bend leading away from Elm Lane the smoke from the chimney fire could be seen sweeping across the road.

"Hose reel, aloft, and two men inside," Barry shouted to us in the crew cab. We disembarked and started to slip and pitch the Ajax Extension Ladder to the roof. Keith had started to get the pump to work prior to us running out the hose reel for whoever was going aloft, when Barry came flying back down the footpath.

"It's a chuffing house fire. Two B.A.'s (Two breathing Apparatus); and get that front door open!" cried Barry. The Ajax Extension Ladder was left to lean against the guttering of the house; Barry and Jack rushed to the front door to try and make and entrance. Verifying it was locked Walt told Jack to link arms, as he needed help to kick the door in. They took five paces back, and then running up the flight of four steps, kicked the door simultaneously. The effect was negative as they were ricocheted back down the steps. "Again!" shouted Walt, and once more Walt and Jack threw themselves at the door, only to be bounced off again.

Looking about me I realised Jack was detailed to wear B.A. that day and Ken had lost his team-mate, so returning to the machine I donned Jack's B.A. and joined Ken at the gateway to take from Keith, the hose reel and gun. I knew I hadn't been passed out as a B.A. wearer for fires, but I had often been told that in fires, rules don't count, and this had all the hallmarks of a good fire. We had just reached the door, with about enough hose reel to enter the house, when the door finally yielded with a loud crack as the lock tore away from the jamb. "Start up," yelled Barry.

My right hand went down to the main valve and I cracked the oxygen cylinder fully open. Inhaling oxygen and exhaling through my nose, I cleared my system of unwanted gases. The nose clips were then put on, and the goggles over my eyes; finally the fire helmet was placed on my head. I was ready! "Keep with me," said Ken, as he ducked down under the smoke layer. Feeding him the hose reel, I followed close behind. We crawled a few feet in and came to the living room door. Ken felt at the door for signs of heat and he nodded in the direction of the door. This was the room involved. Water was still dripping from the hose reel branch test done by Walt. I covered my hand

L-R FM Jim Green, STN.O. Archie Cornish, FM John Parnham, FM Leslie Sawyer
Archie came from a line of fireman, his father was killed whilst serving on job

House fire Elm Lane

with my coat and slowly opened the door. All those hours of training were now making more sense than ever before. As I suspected, as soon as the door catch was released and oxygen allowed into the room, the room exploded into flame. Ken immediately gave a quick splash around, above our heads, to clear burning debris, and into the room where the chairs were burning .I felt a hand tugging at the back of my legs; it was Barry.

"Tell Ken I want you to check upstairs for occupants," Barry gasped. I signalled to Ken that we were required to go upstairs. We crawled back to the door and handed over the hose reel branch to Walt and Jack. Having edged passed them we moved on to the staircase and started our ascent.

"Itsh F-ssching hot," said Ken, side breathing. (When using the oxygen mouthpiece you were not supposed to talk because you let poisonous gas into the system. This meant officially you should only communicate by hand signals, yet often men would disregard communicating by hand signals and talk like Albert Motley doing his ventriloquist act.)

"Oshay," I replied.
As we moved up the stairs it became unbelievably hot and I honestly thought my ears were snirping up (curling up). Ken pressed on through the heat barrier caused by the heat from the fire and the steam from our fire fighting. The immense heat stung the side of my cheeks and I would have turned to go out if it hadn't been for Ken's reassuring comments and occasional tugs on my sleeve. We penetrated through the worst of the heat and lay on the top of the landing where it was cooler.

Ken signalled we were going into the bedroom on my left and we joined hands as we stood up. Ken was on my right hand side as we went into the bedroom. I kept in touch with the wall to my left and with left hand lightly clenched I searched in front of me by the use of a sweeping motion, I also used my feet to test the floor for soundness and obstacles. With Ken to my right using a similar motion we covered half the room in one sweep. In all the times I had done this in the smokehouses at Leeds and Elm Lane, never was it so hot or so humid. The many hours I had toiled under instruction and wondered if Tom Varley's tales were true, I now found understated. Tom's was also correct when he said the first time we had ventilated at the Brigadier's house was nothing to a good house fire, and I believed this to be, as he classed it, 'a good 'un'.

As we searched we ventilated the rooms, which made it more comfortable to work, and soon there was a noticeable drop in the temperature. We went from bedroom to bedroom searching for the occupants of the house, then from below I heard Jack's voice, "There's one here."

Ken and I completed our search upstairs but found nothing. There was still plenty of smoke lingering downstairs as we reported back to Barry that the second floor was clear of fire and casualties.

"Take your sets off and report back here," said Barry.
As we strolled back to the appliance, Ken said, "That was bloody hot, that was," wiping the mucous away from the end of his nose with the back of his hand. The nose clips always seemed to make your nose run, and the hand or the black silk neckerchief, I later found, it was a good substitute for a handkerchief on these occasions. Ken asked me how it felt to wear at my first fatal.

"OK. Up until now. I've still not seen the body." I replied.

It didn't take long to get the B.A. sets off and stored away, along with the miners' helmets and hand lamps that had been worn. Keith, in the meantime, filled us in on how long the fatality had been cooking. The bloke who gave us the 'Running Call', on being told of the death of the old lady, caught a smell of her on Walt's coat and was immediately sick.

With wearing the Salvus I hadn't noticed the sickly sweet smell of burnt flesh that hung about us, and thankfully I was too busy to muse on the situation. We reported back, and Walt asked, "Have you seen her?"
"No," Ken replied, "where is she?"
"Go in and look."

We went, once again, into the living room but it was still heavy with smoke. Then, near to the fireplace, sat in the side chair, was the victim. I didn't see her at first and then something reminiscent of Psycho, the face of the victim, screamed out from a brief break in the smoke haze. I was visually shocked to see the blackened taut features of the woman's skull. Her eyes peered out in a constant gaze that buried deep into your primeval soul. The face had all but disappeared and the once fat had melted away so that the cheeks were sunk into the face, leaving a thin layer of skin covering the bones of the skull. Her lips too had shrunk away, leaving her with the hideous, laughing smile of the dead. With her teeth exposed, a faint trace of blood could be seen around each individual tooth. Her clothing had been partly burnt away, exposing in places her arms and thighs. Where this exposure occurred, the body flesh had all but gone. At some time this woman had borne children out of love, perhaps men had lusted after her in her youth; she was the lovable Grandma that children loved to see at weekends. Now she would be another statistic of a fire fatality.

Barry talked to the Policeman on duty about removing the body after the Police photographer had finished with her. He and Walt had a long discussion on the cause of the fire then told the three of us their suspicions as to the cause. Both opinions were that the old woman had been reading the newspaper in front of the fire, and that she had perhaps fallen asleep and the newspaper fell into the hearth and eventually set fire to the hearthrug. This then smouldered on until it burnt out the living room. I was shown how, by using the varying degrees of burning of the woodwork of the room, you could surmise how the fire had progressed from one piece to the next. Barry pointed out that the light was switched on, so you could say that it was dark when she was doing her reading, thus placing the time between 1900 hours and 0800 hours the following day. On checking the clock we saw that it had stopped at 1000 hours this morning, or 2200 hours last night. Walt asked me if I could tell anything from the windows.

I inspected the glass in the window frames and could see there was a heavy staining with very little crazing, which would indicate a very slow build-up of heat. Also the plaster on the walls was still intact, which is a good indicator that the fire had been a slow build. Jack noticed that the stockings of the late woman had melted in places, with tiny globules of carbon forming at the edges. There was some burnt paper between her legs. With these factors combined, we therefore agreed with Barry's supposition of what had happened, but even if we hadn't I doubt he would have taken any notice.

Walt, since joining the Watch, always went out of his way to encourage us to learn from the fires, or any incident we attended, so that we would have sound knowledge when and if we were promoted. Between the officers on our shift, we the young firemen were growing in stature and the shift was becoming one of the best in the brigade.

The Police eventually released the body and we could then remove it for a post mortem to be carried out by the Police pathologist. As we lifted her up, her bowels gave way, releasing a stench of vile proportions. The flesh on her bones was ready to part so we lifted her with great care onto the salvage sheet before placing her in the metal casket. The state of her body reminded me of a well cooked chicken, when the flesh nearly falls off the bones.

By the time we had done, and cleaned everything used at the fire, it was dinnertime. Try as I might I couldn't rid myself of the smell of the woman's burnt flesh from my skin. We had been thanked by Barry for doing a great job and I was told that from now on I was to be classed as an 'A' wearer, not having to wait four months for the annual B.A. session when the official ratings were given.

On entering the mess room we saw Reaney already tucking into his dinner.
We sat down to eat our meal and Reaney asked Barry about the incident. Barry filled him in on the details of the job and in return asked how his fire prevention task was progressing at Kirk Edge Convent, Worral the local nunnery of the 'Carmelite' nuns. Reaney went into great detail how he and he alone was allowed to walk the hallowed corridors where few men had ever trodden. The Abbess, he was told, would pray for him and I hoped us, for our safekeeping. Albert also told of how the nuns would scurry back into their cells as a young novice went ahead, ringing a bell to warn them of his coming. Reaney loved this adulation that he was one of the chosen few, and jealously made sure that it was he that did all the inspections of the premises.

It was after hearing about Albert's success in saving us all from damnation that we or should I say I, got the true level of our Sub Officer. Elsie, the station's daytime cook, had started to pass out the main course of Roast Beef. As I looked at the plate placed in front of me and saw the medium-rare, red meat, my thoughts once again returned to the fatality of this morning. Jack and Keith intimated that after this morning, it was the least appetising of meals. It was at this point that Barry, grabbed a piece of greasy fat, rolled it to a coil, then placing it to his nose, gave a cough, and let the fat unroll through his hand as though it was an enormous mucous 'Dew drop'. This was all Jack needed to be put off his meal. Mind you, my stomach was not in the mood for this type of sickly joke either.

Under normal circumstances, Reaney would have been on the perpetrator of such a joke like a ton of bricks, but today he said and did nothing. This minor incident only went to prove to me it is not what you know, more of whom you know that gets you by in life. For me my two years had passed and I was now an accepted whole time member of the Sheffield Fire Brigade. Furthermore I was determined I would make Fm. 251 Arthur Levick, one of the firemen who everyone respected, just like Walt Dawes and Tom Varley.

Ass. Div. Officer Albert Reany

Old fire station at Elm Lane

B Spellman, injured fireman at the Wicker fire

Wicker Goods Yard 1966, became in the 1970s Charles Clark Vauxhall dearlership

Wicker Goods Yard 1966, now the site of new Tesco

Events of 1964

Britain and France agree to build a channel tunnel
Winston Churchill leaves the House of Commons for the last time.
Labour win General Election, Harold Wilson Prime Minister.
Start of the swinging sixties, Mary Quant ladies fashion
designer heralds a new dawn when British fashion will lead the World.
Hanging abolished.
Mods (Scooter riders) and Rockers (motor-bike riders) cause
 mayhem by fighting at various holiday towns.

1965
Winston Churchill dies. Britain mourns its Wartime Leader.
Beeching Report, telling of mass Railway closures.
Beatles receive MBEs; some holders hand theirs back.

1966
England win the World Cup.
Aberfan disaster, coal tip slurry buries Welsh village killing 116 children.
Shell/Esso agents Phillips Petroleum strike the biggest gas field off the mouth
of the Humber in the North Sea

Chapter 2

Love, honour, and where is the Exit,

1966-67

The two years since I joined up passed relatively fast, and in that period I tended to think that only I had problems. Although during that time I had some really joyous moments. My girlfriend Janet, within eighteen months of meeting her, we had become man and wife. It was commonly voiced that a rushed relationship was doomed to failure. Yet this five foot, four inches of bleach blonde woman, was everything I desired. Whilst I studied to give myself a career in the brigade, she kept my feet firmly fixed to the ground, and lightened my serious moods with her natural humour. Further to this she gave me a son, Alan.

The mid nineteen sixties were to be years of great changes for the shift, for me the acceptance by Sheffield Fire Brigade had meant job security for the rest of my working life. Although security of where you worked or what station you were sent too, was very much in the hands of the Gods. To say I liked those I worked with would not be an understatement, and the camaraderie that the shift emanated was fantastic. So much so that you wished nothing would change. We had lost Tom for a spell but whilst Barry was on annual leave our beloved 'Biscuit Face' came back has our relief Sub Officer. Dick Ash had been transferred onto Red Watch at Elm Lane after Jim Lambert had complained to Albert Reaney that he was worse off than Tom if service of the all men under them was taken into consideration.

Ken Kendrick and John Horseley's service combined with Dick's five years, made it that one of them had to be transferred instead of me, Richard lost. Well when I say lost, that is not exactly true, since they (Horseley and Ash) had found out that Parker, Rosier, Kendrick, and I had all caught them up with promotional exams. They suddenly took up their studying in earnest once again, and for Richard there would be no more sideways moves, only promotional ones.

The daylight hours got shorter as winter months drew on, and all appeared well in the garden of life. Perhaps this is why chimera, waits until it lulls you into a false sense of security before striking.

Elsie had begun to put out the dinner when we received a fire call. Tom and Reaney ran to the Watchroom and, as we sat getting ready in the cab, it was obvious that it was something special as they looked at the Master Street Plan for confirmation of something connected with the call. As Albert came out of the Watchroom he shouted to Keith to transfer his kit to the station van and to act as his runner and message carrier.

Tom told John the address of the incident and it became all too clear why the officers were concerned. The local gas plant at Barrow Road was on fire and flames were spreading back to the main gasholders, which held around 100,000 cubic feet of town gas. If these exploded the blast would demolish several square miles of residential and industrial properties and kill God knows how many people. The gas works were in our area and we were soon in attendance at the incident. Reaney had sped off ahead at different times during the journey to the works to make sure we had a clear passage at busy road junctions, and Keith said, "He frightened the hell out of me at times with his driving."

On arrival at the incident we were met by the plant manager who didn't take long to explain the danger we were all in. The Gas Plant consisted of two gasholders with their production retorts, purification and enrichment buildings, which covered about a quarter of a square mile of land in the bottom of the Wincobank Hill. From the plant entrance on the left were the security and administrative buildings and two hundred and fifty feet further in, the laboratories that were overshadowed by the gasholders. To the right were the retorts and other gas manufacturing and distribution buildings. To the north of the plant were the train lines that supplied the coal for the retorts and to the southeast was the main Leeds to Sheffield passenger railroad cutting. A twenty-four inch distribution main passed from the gasholder, over the laboratories, then down the rear of and in between the pumping house and the old L.N.E.R. railway track heading south towards Sheffield industrial basin. Further pipes criss-crossed the plant taking steam, which was mixed with Naphtha, over a catalyst to enrich the calorific value of the gas and other associated processes to create the town gas we used.

The section of the distribution main involved was approximately 100 yards away from the number two gasholder and flames were endangering the purification buildings, which would eventually include the Naphtha storage tank area. The fire had been caused through an accident when a mobile crane crashed its boom into the pipeline creating a fracture and a fire.

Reaney immediately got us to set up a series of cooling jets to protect the buildings and the gasholders. Fire appliances from the fire stations of Darnall, Rocko' and Mansfield Road also attended, plus the new hydraulic Merryweather Turntable Ladder (T.T.L.) from Rocko' and the old mechanical one from Darnall. Like all major incidents, it took time for all the appliances to arrive and to be placed in their best operational position. We, being the first in attendance were 'got to work' on cooling the buildings near to the burning main. Yet it didn't take the Senior Officer long to countermand the orders of Reaney, and our new orders were to play our jet onto the main on the supply side of the holder.

Meanwhile Ken and Jack had got the water from a nearby street hydrant into the pump for John, and had subsequently run out another hose line and got a second jet to work to cut off the radiant heat from the city side of the burning main. Whilst this was going on the crews from the other stations got into the street water mains and the Shiregreen Brook for their supplies, using the Lightweight Pumps off the Wr.T.s to get the diminished autumn / winter water of the brook onto the gas main. As already said, the appliances arrived piece meal at a fire and pumps are invariably sited in the wrong location because of this. So when Divisional Officer Frank Peel arrived at the incident he found two T.L.s with just about sufficient water supply to keep them operational, various other jets being played onto buildings that didn't need protecting and badly positioned branch crews soaking each other with their respective jets.

Varley and Reaney had ordered that the Mansfield Road crew set into position the water supply to feed the foam protection installation on the Naphtha tanks. This system was installed in an adjacent building to the tanks marked 'P.F.D.' (Petroleum Flash Distillation), and had its own pump, foam supply and fixed foam pourers; consequently all that was needed was the water for the foam solution. This should have been a simple enough task to complete, but the sign that had been erected to show how the system worked was numbered wrong. Instead of water going just to the main inlet valve it was now going directly into the foam solution storage tank and a watery foam solution was seeping from under the door, when Tom went to check how they were doing. Spotting what was going wrong he shut down the offending valve and opened up the correct one, thus stopping the situation from getting worse.

"How much water got into the solution?" queried Tom?
"No idea," was the reply. "Well how long have you been pumping water into

Barrow Road Gas Works

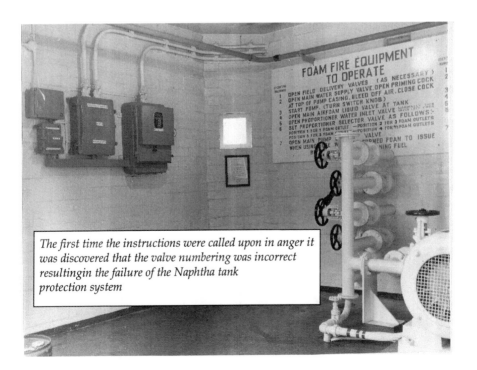

The first time the instructions were called upon in anger it was discovered that the valve numbering was incorrect resulting in the failure of the Naphtha tank protection system

this system?" asked Tom.

"Dunno! About three minutes, maybe," came the reply from the Mansfield Road Sub Officer. "Well let's hope we don't need it," remarked Tom as he left.

Tom reported to the D.O. of the foam/Naphtha situation and wheels were set in motion to get the emergency foam stock from Elm Lane. The incident had now been going for twenty minutes and with the knocking off of superfluous jets and the start of resiting the T.L.s (Turntable Ladders) the job had entered its critical stage.

The Gas Management had started to cut off and isolate the main involved from the rest of the installation. It was decided to simultaneously extinguish both the exterior and the interior flames. Workmen were frantically trying to get an inspection cover off the main, before the gas pressure in the pipe was reduced to such an extent that it would allow the gas flame to burn back into the holder and thereby cause an explosion. With the last of the bolts loosened on one of the covers, it was expected that the extinguishing of the flames was imminent. Ken and I had been detailed to extinguish the interior flame when it was exposed, but in the meantime our task was to keep the gas main cool from buckling and distorting, causing further leaks. Ken was the first to notice that the flame had gone back further than the inspection cover being removed and was now burning around one of the adjoining flanges further down towards the holders. At first the plant engineer said it was impossible, because the pressure supplied by the lifts of the holder was sufficient to keep the gas burning well away from the holders. I was beginning to understand why firemen don't trust the experts in any particular field, when Ken said, "For God's sake, look there."

The flames were now licking back to another flange joint and at the rate of burn back we had only ten minutes before the whole works went up and us with it. You would expect at that stage for a slight panic to ascend on everybody, but it didn't. The gas workmen ran back to the penultimate flange and started to release the bolts. The only order of retreat was given to the two monitor operators on the T.L.s to fix jets to provide a water curtain for the exposed buildings they were protecting. With the monitors fixed the men started to descend their respective ladders. I must admit that at this time I thought, "You've made a crap decision joining this lot, Arthur," and to quote the Earl of Cardigan when he led the 'Charge of the Light Brigade', "Here goes the last of the Brudenells." I in turn thought, "This is the last of the youngest Levick's."

How long it took the Gas workforce I can't say, but there started a hissing sound issuing from the last main flange joint and my eyes fixed on it, along with everyone else, for the sign of a flame. Just then someone shouted, "it's nearly off, get ready!"

Ken kept the jet playing along the gas main right up and until the inspection plate dropped off, exposing the internal space of the twenty four-inch diameter pipe. With a smooth movement of the jet we extinguished the internal fire and the crew from Darnall Road did the same to the external one. It was out, but the danger from re-ignition from residue hot spots remained. Then Tom ordered that the main be purged from the bank of CO_2 (Carbon Dioxide) extinguishers he had positioned standing close by played into the gas main until the plant manager said, "The supply is shut down."

For a moment or two we still played out jets of water onto the main in the hope of over kill, then we shut them down. We had won! After the make-up we returned to our station. Reaney and Keith went around assisting back-up stations, returning equipment they had left behind when their appliances returned to their home bases. Ken was telling Tom that today proved what he had always thought; men from other stations should become more involved with fire risks in their own and neighbouring station areas that they are likely to attend. Tom agreed and said he would broach the matter with Reaney at the first opportunity. Whilst we had our bit of excitement for the day, unknown to us our next call was being prepared.

A young married couple, on returning from work to Vauxhall Road, Wincobank, found a strong smell of gas as they drove closer to home. When they arrived at their home the smell of gas was so strong that they had not gone inside but had gone to a telephone kiosk to call out the gas board to a suspected leak. The gas repair man arrived within ten to fifteen minutes, which was pretty quick considering the amount of calls had been made since the area's gas supply was cut off during fire fighting operations. The Police had toured the area at the time, warning people to shut off their gas appliances until further notice and as soon as it was safe they were to repeat the act, giving them the all clear. This worked out reasonably well for those who were at home during the gas incident, but our young couple were at work and had no intimation of what had gone off during the afternoon.

The gas board workman told the couple of the gas shut-off and in return the young couple told him they had left several gas fires burning on a low setting when they went to work.

31

"That'll account for the build-up of gas in your house," he said as he walked into their home, "don't light up yet; I'll check it out for you," he continued. The husband either didn't hear or misheard the remark for when he followed the other two into the room he automatically switched on the light.

FLASH! BANG! WALLOP!

They say time flies and it certainly does in an explosion. The household's clock, along with the wife and gasman, were blown out through the window; the husband was blown out through the open door.

Once again we were hurtling down Newman Road to Wincobank, finally arriving at the demolished house. The fire was soon extinguished and the three occupants, at the time of the explosion, were not before too long winging their way to the burns unit of the City General Hospital. We made the premises safe and I was amazed at how little damage was visible at first sight. Apart from the missing window you'd have thought they had escaped with very little damage but if you looked across the floor you would notice the wooden floor was at a slightly raised angle, and the absence of furniture. The floor at some point had lifted sufficiently with the blast and emptied the contents of the living room into the cellar, although there was hardly a scratch mark on the walls to show that this had happened.

We returned to base, thinking how many more gas related fires before this shift ends. Even when we were in the engine house and cleaning off the appliance, we were all on edge ready for our next call.

The following day when the events of the last 24 hours had truly sunk in, Jack asked Walt," What was the scariest hair raising fire you've been too?" Thinking like me that yesterday's incident would be his choice, we were taken aback by his answer when he said that, "No incident had ever scared him, but it was the 'Flowerdays' wood yard incident that he was aware of the danger he was in. The building had lost its floors and this left high walls which might collapse onto him, and being crushed hadn't ever appealed to him."

For us young firemen yesterday was as close as I want to get again to seeing the Grim Reaper waiting quietly in the wings, for us to join him. If I thought my life had its moments then it must be added that my brother Keith could also lay claims to that statement. Keith had joined the Police Force in 1963 and Police Constable Pc.747, life dealing with the general public likewise had its adrenaline encounters.

I can remember Keith could have hardly served more than a year when whilst on patrol he spotted several men working on the roof of the Royal Infirmary Hospital. Now any normal being would not have given the men a second glance, but Keith it rang alarm bells in his head. He observed the men for several minutes and it came apparent to him that they were stripping the roof of its lead covering. In today's Police Force the Constable would ask for back up on his radio but in 1964 personal radios were a thing to come. So he withdrew his whistle and gave several loud blasts, which was the signal for any other Constable hearing it to come to his assistance. The only trouble with that way of communicating was that the offenders also heard the whistle, and tried to make good their escape. Yet lead is not the easiest or the lightest material to carry, never mind run with. Fortunately for Keith his best mate heard his warning call and was able to ring from the Police telephone kiosk that a Constable was in trouble in the area of the hospital. It took a little time for help to arrive yet it was sufficient for Keith and his mate Alan to arrest several of the offenders whilst a Police mobile apprehended the lorry carrying the lead. This would have been a good feather in his cap, especially since he was still a recruit. Yet this arrest he gave to his pal because he hadn't achieved his target of apprehensible offences.

Keith was a natural beat copper; he had an enquiring mind and basically he trusted no one, a good lesson for any copper to learn. Yet like me he loved this uniformed life we led. In fact all my family, that is mother and brother and myself, served in emergency services: Mum was a nurse, Keith and I as stated. It had become obvious to us that these services gave you a secure future and living.

Although Keith missed out on that arrest, a short while later he brought into custody a man who had been causing chaos on Rutland Road. You may ask how can one man create havoc with the morning rush hour traffic. The answer is very simple, especially when he is dressed has a woman who kept leaping from his house and rushing out into the road and exposing himself to the drivers.

It was the man's pleas when arrested that showed my brothers good nature for he allowed him to cover over his dress with man's apparel so as not to cause him further embarrassment. This soft spot caused him also to get his first black eye, when helping a drunk outside the Dial House pub to get dressed after defecating in the street. The man thumped him when he tried to help him get dressed again.

On the following morning when the man had sobered up and appeared in court with some facial bruising claiming Police rough handling. It was the magistrate who commented, "Your bruises compared with officer are minor; furthermore if you are incapable of controlling your motions perhaps it is feasible that you couldn't control your walking actions either. Perhaps it was as the Constable stated you staggered into a lamp post."

Experience never came cheap and over the year both Keith and I learnt what it meant to serve the public. So as the years rolled by we became more and more seasoned veterans. If I thought my biggest battle had been fought one evening in the late sixties I discovered that was not true.

The Pump Escape had gone into the workshops for its service and we had got Rocko's spare Dennis/Escape. Ken hated the brute and was having difficulty getting the gears has it had the crash-box type. Tom told him if he liked he could take it for another familiarisation run around the station area. On his return to the station he still wasn't happy with it. Although Ken was having trouble driving this vehicle, to us it appeared the evening would be a quiet one, but one thing about this job is that you never know what to expect. It is this aspect that I like so much; you can never totally relax. Yet this evening I don't think any of us had any inclination of what was to be a long night.

That evening two lorries containing Naphtha found themselves parked up on Sussex Road awaiting off loading at the Effingham Road Gas works. What happened officially was never truly fathomed but the accepted theory was that the brakes of the fixed tanker containing 500 gallons (2250 L) failed and rolled back into the second trailer tanker containing 1000 gallons (4500 L).

On night's like these if anything can go wrong it will. Regardless of why, and how, it did happen. Nothing is more certain than no one saw the tanker slowly rolling back, until it was too late. Admittedly the impact force wasn't great but the weight of the vehicle was sufficient for the fixed tanker to puncture its load on the front of the tractor cab of the vehicle behind. It was Sod's, maybe Murphy's Law or whoever you wish to credit for the accident. Still, one positive fact which cannot be denied was that just a few feet away from both tankers was a new road works project with its night paraffin lamps guarding a hole. Fuel spilled out of the tanker trickled a few feet before coming into contact with an open flame of the lamps.

It was the initial explosion that so shocked the lady operating the public weighbridge; she fell over and broke her leg. The drivers were helpless to extinguish the flames although they did separate the vehicle enough so that we did have a chance, even though it was only slight.

It is on nights like these you trust your offices, furthermore you obey any orders without question. He hasn't time to explain why he does a thing; the time to question him is after, and hope that it makes sense to you has it did to him. We got called out on the initial shout along with Rocko, Darnall and Mansfield Road.

Ken cleared the engine house when he first crunched the gears, and this seemed to make him lose his confidence in his driving ability. We kangarooed to the main road junction before descending down the steep Barnsley Road that led into Sheffield. All the way down, Ken failed to find the gears, and on reaching the bottom at Fir Vale, had now to climb the other side of the valley hill. Ken tried, but once the vehicle was moving, he couldn't catch the second gear, so we hopped once more up the initial slope of Barnsley Road leading into Sheffield.

"What's up Ken?" said Tom.
"I can't get second on this thing."
"Go on, make it have it," urged Tom.
"You have a go if you think it's easy," replied Ken.

With that the two exchanged places. Tom was known in the past for his fast driving, but I'd never seen him drive whilst I had been on the job. He was credited for blowing up two engines when driving to incidents, and now I was going to witness myself, the master of fire engine driving. Vrooom and click as he slid into first, and with another burst of revs he pushed into second. With each gear the appliance picked up speed. Vrooom, third, and we were sill accelerating when we reached the top of Burngreave Road. Now what lay before us was about a mile descent into Sheffield. From the brow of the hill we could see the glow of fire reflecting back off the evening clouds.

Faster and faster we accelerated, 40, 50, 60 mph. the engine screamed its delight as we descended like a bat out of hell. There are few occasions that I have seen men brace themselves in the back. The one that stands out was when Terry Smith drove us to Bassetts sweet factory early one summer's morning. As we tore down the hill of Penistone Road towards Owlerton, it was usual for the drivers to take a wide sweep onto the opposite carriageway to take the sharp left-hand bend at the bottom, if possible. But this particular morning, although the road was clear of traffic, he stayed well onto his own carriageway, even though he was picking up speed as he approached the bend.

Five early morning fishermen were sat on their baskets waiting outside Sheffield United Tours booking office, for their coach to arrive. When all of a sudden, out of nowhere as far as they were concerned, (we hadn't been using the bell because it was too early), a red lorry came into view, skidding broadside on as it tried to negotiate the corner opposite them.

As we approached the bend, all hands grasped for the internal strengthening pole in the centre of the crew cab as, like in the children's game 'climbing hands', the crew tried to secure a grip to help brace themselves when we looked like going into the booking office. Terry fortunately regained control and just managed to stop the appliance bumping into the opposite kerb edge. As we sped away we looked in the vehicle mirror, and all we could see was ten legs sticking up in the air as the owners of the baskets had fallen backwards to escape being hit by the red devil.

As Tom sped through the last set of traffic lights before the Gas Works, we were still bracing ourselves from the journey down the hill. Then, just ahead of us, were the taillights of Rocko's Escape, slopping water as she raced on. We had made up the time lost and even gained some. For us to be so close to Rocko's appliance, which had only two thirds of the distance to travel, God knows what actual speed we must have travelled at to get there.

Tom parked up at the rear of the growing line of appliances and was immediately contacted by D.O. Peel who had just completed his first inspection of the fire ground.

"Take your crew and Foam equipment, Tom, and help out 'Danks' with the Naphtha tankers, and get one of your chaps to go and man the L.P.P." (Lightweight Portable Pump)

We collected all the foam making equipment from our appliance and each man, laden to the full, started the short journey to Darnall's Water Tender we thought to be just around the corner in Sussex Road. Keith was leading the way followed by Jack and myself; each carrying four gallons of foam compound in cans with their identity discs in the handles that cut into the hands. The discs were there to help you differentiate between the petrol cans and the foam in the dark. On turning into the street we were confronted with a Naphtha tanker burning away and one jet snaking wildly across the road. We all dropped our cans and started to regain control of the unmanned branch. Keith and I crawled our way up the length of the hose slowly, pinning it down and eventually bringing it under control.

Tom told us to put up a protective water screen between the tanker and the works, then he sent Jack back to find out which pump was supplying our jet and to have it knocked off so that we could insert our No 2 F.M.B But before Jack could carry out his order he changed his mind and grabbed hold of Furniss.

"Get me the Monitor Branch with the largest nozzle we carry, I'll emulsify this bastard lot," he bellowed. Jack turned on his heels once more and ran back to our appliance.
"You two O.K.," shouted Tom. Keith nodded our reply.

"I'm just going up here to see what's going on," he said,"I'll be back in a minute."
"What the hell are you two doing," a voice questioned from the back of us just as Tom disappeared from view. It was Assistant Divisional Officer Harry Hibbert from Darnall.

"I told you to play that Jet onto the Holder," he commanded.

We tried to explain to him but he moved off refusing to hear our plea. So we placed the jet of water onto the Holder sides cooling down the exposed area "What have I just told you, put that Jet onto the Tankers," commanded Peel who was as we could see following in Hibbert's footsteps. So once more we turned our Jet to provide a water curtain between tankers and gas-holder. Mr. Peel also refused to let us explain Mr. Hibbert's request.

"Are you F---ing stupid, I told you to put that jet onto the holder, we have an office block going as well," Hibbert remonstrated once more as he toured the fire ground like Peel. I looked at Parker and he looked at me, we knew it was pointless to argue so we carried out the last order given.

Thankfully Tom returned and told me when Jack arrived to go back to the supply pump and give as much pressure of water as he could have, a hundred pounds per square inch, at least.

As soon as Jack appeared and settled himself as Parker's back up I left to carry out Tom's wishes. Tracing the hose was comparable with searching for the end of a strand of spaghetti in a bowl. Taking care not to lose the line of hose I required, I finally found myself at the rear of Darnall's Pump Escape with Ron Griffiths manning the pump. Ron told me in no uncertain language that he couldn't comply with Tom's request. So I therefore ran to Ken and organised the line to be fed from our pump. After much running about I finally returned to our band manning the inch and one-eighth nozzle. This branch has it is termed was capable of knocking down a man or even lifting a man completely off the ground, and with high pressure ordered by Tom it would be quite an handful for four men. In no time at all we had suppressed and extinguished the fire on both tankers. This left only the fires in the office block and the gas main feeding the street lamp to extinguish. These were also taken care of in the course of the night. Now if we had questioned Varley or senior officer what he did, why he did, today's landscape around Sheffield might look a lot different.

Varley told me later that he soon realised that the foam he had wasn't sufficient to coat both tankers. It was a gamble how long we had before either of the tankers exploded and if that happened there was a definite possibility that the holder would go soon after. This danger I can confirm because at one point during the night I was one of the message runners for Peel and I had to relay to him the message from the main gas board engineer. "That he wouldn't come any further nearer to the works than the Wicker Arches, for safety reasons." He also said, " that if the site went up a quarter of Sheffield would soon join it." The risk was not only from the tanker but the Naphtha that had got into the drains. We sat that night pumping water into the drains and all Sheffield emergency services worked as one. For eight hours we sat on a potential time bomb. The orders that were given might have been better, if we had the use of more available Foam, if we had some means of confining the Naphtha to the area surrounding the tankers, the danger wouldn't have been as great. You can always fight a fire better with hindsight, but it is a gift only given to commentators of incidents never to the man in charge.

We trusted Tom and had faith that our officers knew what they were about; it never crossed our minds at the time that we should disobey an order because we didn't understand or agree.

A Postscript to this fire happened months later at the quarterly Chief Officers' and Fire Brigade Union meeting that the incident was brought up.

"I had a letter from 'The Mayor' the other week and he and the council as a whole, wish to say thank you to the Brigade by erecting a plaque to the people involved," said Lambert.

"Will this be added to the men's personal records?" asked Terry Perkins.
"Why?" asked Lambert?
"Well, it would be appreciated that at future job interviews that this gives a guidance to the quality of the man," replied Terry.
"I sent my reply to the Mayor, on receiving this letter, saying that we thanked them for the offer made but we were only doing our duty," Lambert said emphatically.

"It was more than just duty," challenged Terry.
"Mr. Troy!" shouted Lambert.

Troy the Brigade Secretary, had been taking notes, and the calling of his name shocked him, as he couldn't think why he was being dragged into this row.

"Yes, Mr. Lambert," he said peering over his nose end glasses.
"Why weren't the men paid last month?" asked Lambert.
"They were!" retorted Troy.
"And the men who attended there who were volunteers?" queried Lambert.
"The fire service personnel were all 'on duty men' at the actual incident. A.D.O. Albert Reaney and the personnel living in the flats at Division Street made up an appliance for the use of the City, but it wasn't needed."
"So what you are saying is that all the men who attended that incident were being paid to be firemen; that is apart from the gas board workers and the Police, who again were being paid to do their job."
"Yes."
"And therefore nobody there was a volunteer."

Turning back to our union delegation he added, "why on earth should you be rewarded for doing your duty? You don't tip your doctor for prescribing medicines to you. Do you? Lambert stubbed out his own rolled up apology for a cigarette with vigour. The letter of thanks was made known to the Brigade but nothing was ever added to the men's records who fought the fire that night, and no plaque was ever raised in their honour - which I always thought was a pity.

We had just finished the evening drill session and the appliances were still on the drill ground, when two young ladies walked across from the nearby doctor's surgery. It was apparent from their conversation that the two women were foreigners. After standing off a while, one of the ladies approached me.

"It is a not er possible that we take photograph at side of fire engine?" said the young woman, in broken English. Now I was not knocking how she talked, for I can only speak one other language besides my native tongue, and that is fluent gibberish.

"Yes luv, by all means take your photograph," I said. The girl took out from her bag an old concertina type of camera. Looking at the camera inquisitively, she looked across to her companion and spoke to her in what sounded like Russian. A short conversation took place then the lady walked over to me once more.

"I borrow from my uncle thees camera, but nit know how it vorks," she laughed.
"Well I'm no photographer myself, but I'll see if I can get someone to help," I looked at the woman and hoped she understood.

The crews had been watching and were inquisitive to know what they wanted. I filled them in on the needs of the young woman and finished by saying, "So who knows about cameras?"

We walked back over to the two women and I explained very slowly in the best tradition of an Englishman communicating with anybody from across the Channel, that Ken who spoke a little Russian through his son being a Russian translator would take their photo's.

Ken examined the camera and altered the apertures and speed settings, then by hand gestures, moved the women into the frame of the picture. After several photos were taken, the woman asked, "Could er we look inside?"

Once more I complied with our visitors request. The tight skirt she wore needed hitching as she climbed into the cab, revealing her thighs.

"Could you er have photograph with both of us?" she asked in her heavy Russian accent. I was about to decline when Ken shouted to Keith to come and have his photograph taken.

Ken took pictures of the four of us; the ladies being lifted in and out of the machines because of the skirts they wore; and after a few minutes was satisfied that he had got on film what the women wanted.

"You be so kind. In Poland it not possible to photo fireman. We thank you so much very," she said demurely, "and can I take one of all of you, to show my family back home?"

The crew were assembled and a photograph taken, and with promises that they would send thanks to the C.F.O, they departed. I thought no more about our Polish visitors until one evening about a week later, when Janet returned home fuming.

"What do you lot get up to at that place?" she asked.
"Er, you've lost me love," I queried, sensing that a normally static object was about to come flying in my direction.
"How many women have you had your hands on today?"
"None," I cried with conviction.
"Your hands are so varm I feel zem thru my skirt," she mimicked.

All the alarm bells started ringing in my head as I realised that the two young ladies had set me up, or us. What had they told Janet about that photograph session? The young women were of actual Polish decent, and Linda Stephansky worked with Janet at the shop in Sheffield. She told of how they had been to the doctors for some minor ailment and on coming out had seen the fire engines. They wondered if we would let them take photographs at close quarters, so they put on the act of visitors. Linda told the rest of the staff at Sheffield of how helpful we were and how many photographs she had of the firemen stationed there, and she passed them out for the staff to see.

"I was looking at Linda's sister, then the next photo she showed me was of you with her," Janet snapped. A silent curse went out to Linda from my mind. I was in a no win situation. I could hardly deny they were of the lads, and me but would she believe me that nothing happened. I decided to throw myself on her mercy and tried to remember which casualty department would be opened tonight.

Again, the one who sees all smiled down on me, and Janet accepted the truth that we had only assisted what we thought were visitors to this country, and the matter was dropped. I resolved from then on to ask for passport proof if asked to have my picture taken with a stranger again.

They say life is one long learning curve and I am now beginning to believe that to be true; if I am increasing my fire knowledge daily I am also learning very much more about people. All the officers say, " that we are a public service and servants to the public."

This was never greater shown to me than an incident we had at Lamb Drive some months ago. Varley was in charge of a grass fire backing onto that locality. Our initial attack was with beaters but a wind change caused that action to be inadequate. Keith Parker and I managed to jump through the flame that sprung back into life in the scrubland vegetation. It was obvious to both Parker and I that Varley, Kendrick, Smith, and Furniss were now been driven back toward the old Wadsley Bridge brickyard quarry edge.

Varley yelled to Keith and I, " to get the hose reel to work off the machine."

As I looked back Varley had gathered the crew to work along side him, we in the meantime raced back for the appliance. On reaching the estate houses of Lamb Drive we both realised we had run further up than we originally entered the fray, and instead of a trampled down fence we were met by old rusting metal railings. Parker tried to raise himself up onto the railings only to suffer from the pointed bar impaling into his palms. Dropping back he asked me, " to give him a leg up."

This I did and once over let him rush to Horseley for the hose reel and life saving water. I in turn was to follow, only I decide to rap my neckerchief around one hand for a little protection. On gaining the top of the railings I discovered that my boots became wedged in the spacing between the bars. Try as I may I couldn't release myself, and now it was all up to Parker and Horseley to save the Blue Watch crew. A group of women watched my predicament and slowly came down their garden path to see me struggle. Seeing a young mother I asked her, " If she would come forward for me to balance myself so that I could step out of my boots." She came forward and I went to rest my arm on her shoulder only for her to turn and tell me to, " Piss off."

Now clowns like Little Tich could raise themselves back to the vertical when leaning at thirty degrees, but I am not Little Tich. As she backed away I crashed over but my feet were still firmly fixed between the railings, a searing pain shot through my body and I went for a short time unconscious. Whilst I hung upside down on the railing the women were convulsed in hysterical laughter. Once or twice when conscious came upon me my eyes witnessed these cackling witches. Keith meanwhile managed to get water to our beleaguered crew.

Sometime later Varley, Jack and Keith helped me to the ground. A hospital visit on our way back to the Station revealed that I had severely sprained both ankles and I was told that fireman don't go off sick with injuries, they take over light duties in the Watchroom.

Years later I would regret this move but it taught me that their employers never respect servants, and that was a lesson I should have learnt years ago.

Events of 1967
A new city to be built north of London called "Milton Keynes."
Colin Campbell dies trying to break world water speed record on Coniston Waters in his speedboat BlueBird.
Breathalyser introduced by Police to try and stop drunk driving.

P.C Keith Levick

Chapter 3

1968

You had to laugh or cry.

Changes in personnel were always the start to the New Year and in addition we are ordered that all personnel with less than five years are to be sent to Rocko on all occasions to gain firefighting and special appliance experience. This added to the changes involving by men being promoted or just because the Chief liked to swap men around. This was a throw back in history to when men were recruited from ex sailors. The aim of the then navy was to stop cliques forming. Jim Smith was one from our batch of recruits who has resigned from the service because he cannot afford to stop on the low wages. He has now gone back into the tool making industry, but says he can now at least feed his family without getting help from his mother.

Bert Rosier is also to leave us. He has applied for a job in Cambridgeshire as a fireman and has been told he has a better chance of promotion there. This I doubt as he is well thought of by the senior officers here. In his place we are to get Peter Cawthorne, an ex-Navy bloke who served on the aircraft carrier, HMS Bulwark, so we will have some fresh stories to hear. The new sub officer, after several temporary postings, has finally been installed and guess who it is?

Barry Jones.

Since doing the union job I have become aware of the unofficial deals that go on between the C.F.O. and the Union officials. Some of them are not to the benefit of the brigade as a whole; more as a benefit to some individual.
Station Officer Trooper Sinclair is to go to Darnall and Arthur Unwin is to be transferred here in his place.

"Dan Troops," as we affectionately knew him, did his national service in the Royal Marines, and he transferred that service's idiosyncrasies to his men. We were never Firemen; we were always referred to as Trooper Parker, Trooper Lev. He never managed to finish the last three letters of my name all the time he was up here. It was, "Get the ol' watsit, over the ol' thingy, one troop aloft. It your baby Lev."

Our Leading fireman Bud Roberts and later on Walt Dawes would translate it back into English for us.

"Ajax ladder pitched to the roof, one line of hose aloft, taken by Fireman Levick."

Arthur Unwin is a leader of the Queen's Adventure Scouts and had decided we are physically sloppy, so he has introduced a compulsory training programme based on the Canadian Parachute Regiment. Most have taken to it, but once again I find myself balking at the compulsory side of it. We are expected to do PT. then go straight out and do drill for two hours. If only they would let us give voluntary of our time and ask what we would like to do. It never has occurred to them that a sweetener with the medicine makes it easier to take. Unwin has taken it for granted that he can treat us like the teenagers he leads in the scouts and has acquired the nickname of 'Mr. Scoutmaster'.

I have never been averse to studying although I prefer to do such work on my own, and whilst doing relief duties at Rocko this view has been reinforced more. It was on our first night when Brian Marsden who has started to study again for his 'O' levels, because like myself hadn't attained any whilst at school. I don't know why, but there are several members of the Brigade, at this present time, studying for different 'O' and 'A' levels, and I have to admire them as I find it hard to study for the work related exams, never mind anything extra.

So this shift has become a seeker of knowledge and fountain of wisdom with its inevitable question and answer sessions. On the one hand you have Brian with actual 'O' level questions, and on the other you have Stan Jones and John Haig taking questions out of magazines as their General Knowledge questions. One such evening, we were sat around the mess room table when Brian started the question session.

"Who was Hailey Sell-ale?"
Blank looks swept across our faces. Who was Hailey Sell-ale?
After a suitable pause, Brian filled us in on the answer.
"Hailey Sell-ale is better known to his people as the 'Lion of Judea'.
"You f---ing dipstick. That is pronounced Haile Selassie and he was the Emperor of Ethiopia," interrupted Jim Green.
With much laughter John put forward the next question.
"I am sixteen years old and I am engaged to this sailor with a wooden leg. What should I do?"
"Aunty Mary advises that you break it off," replied Woody.

"My turn, my turn," said John, "Dear Doctor Simms, I have been suffering from Pleg-ham," he then looked round the table and asked, "What the bloody hell is Pleg-ham?"

I snatched the paper out of his hand and read the Doctor's column. "It's Phlegm," shaking my head in disbelief. I don't know how they are going to go on when the exam comes, but I should love to see their answer papers. It was at times like these that a tactical withdrawal was deemed necessary and I would creep away, leaving John and his squeaky voice reading out another question.

"Did you know that the largest earth moving digger could shift, in its bucket, the surface area of a football pitch?"
"And that same Digger has got a billiard table installed in the top of its gear-shift lever," a voice would interrupt.
Yes, studying in the fire service was best done away from the place, for sanity's sake

One of the calls we have received this month was to a brothel, and a greater set of ugly bags I have yet to see. The 'Madam' of the household gave you the impression that her face was modeled on a bag of spanners. The calls of late have been very much a routine affair; this one is set apart because of its occupants, not the actual fire.

We got the call at 1755 hours and were mobilised to the growing Asian and West Indian quarter of Sheffield called Pitsmoor. This once had been where the elite of Sheffield City's Industrialists lived in their large mansion style housing dating back to 1846. Yet with the industrial revolution, created by these gents, they eventually had to move out to the rural suburbs of Sheffield, leaving their large majestic properties to become ravaged by time and wars.
It was to one of these large houses that we were now mobile. On arriving, it was obvious that the chimney was on fire and we swung into action with the ease of a well-oiled machine. The fire was tackled from the top and I was now as much up top as I was inside at these incidents, for Keith, Jack and myself would race to go aloft, treating it as a perk.

The fire was quickly extinguished and we started to make up our equipment. Barry asked me to check the roof void of the house. This was a matter of routine, to see if the structure of the chimney was sound and that there were no bricks missing that would allow hot soot to escape and build up on the loft floor, which might ignite the timbers of the roof void. I had just positioned the short extension ladder to the hatch leading into the loft when I saw into one of the women's' rooms. It was not as you would have imagined; no frilly pink lace curtains; or soft pastel colours on the bedding; nothing as seen in movies about whores. The room was virtually clear of furniture apart from a bed and an open tallboy with the occupant's clean and dirty clothing falling out of it opened drawers. On the bed was soiled bed linen that hadn't been washed for weeks. A young woman sprawled herself over this grubby heap, chewing away on some gum. Children's comics were strewn all over the floor and part of the bed. A ceramic chamber pot was visible under the bed, along with discarded underwear.

"Do some 'at special for blokes in uniform," she offered to Jack or me.
"I wouldn't touch her with thy prick ne'er mind mine," said Jack to me.
On completion of our task we made up the ladder and returned it to the machine. Barry came out, following the young girl from upstairs, carrying a load of chipped crockery full of tea.
"She asked if you'd like a drink," said the girl.
Behind her Barry made as if to vomit, then said, "Of course they would. Here Arthur," as he offered me a tea stained, chipped mug. The girl stood as we each took a mug, and waited until we had drunk of the brew.
"Go on, have a drink," egged on Barry.
"I'll wait until I get home," said Walt, replacing the mug onto the tray. The others followed suit, but as I, the last, was about to return the cup, Barry said, "Don't be ungrateful; at least have a sip, and that's an order!"
I took the briefest sip and replaced the mug back on the tray.
"Sorry luv, can't stop any longer; got to get back. Give my thanks to Mrs. Proctor. We'll be going," Barry said, backing to the machine.
When she left, I spat out the tea and swore to myself; Barry was on my hit list to return his favour. They say elephants never forget; and neither do I.

It was the following tour and I was doing relief duty down at "Rocko" (a name retained from the mid-nineteen twenties, when appliances from the old station turned out onto Rockingham Street, before the new one, which turned out onto Division Street), for the full shift. The weather had turned from rain to snow and we had spent the first morning putting on 'skid chains' so that the vehicles could negotiate the hills around Sheffield. There then followed a brief break in the weather and it started to thaw, so we removed them only to find that around 1530 hours it started to snow heavily and once more they had to be put back on. This was always a cold and messy job, especially since the skid chains were stored in a mixture of paraffin and oil to stop them corroding.

Our first call was to the old isolation hospital, at Lodge Moor, which still specialised in the treatment of chest ailments, and spinal injuries.

As in most cases when you get a call through the automatic fire detection system in a hospital, it was a false alarm. The back up appliances from the predetermined attendance were sent back after the 'stop message' was sent and we were detailed to go around the nearby risks and remove any snow from the fire hydrants that served them. This was an easy task but we hadn't gone a quarter of a mile when a link snapped off the skid chains. We had just finished removing the offending links when we got a further special service call. A child was under a bus in the heart of the city. The race to the city was a noisy one, for as we travelled the skid chain disintegrated and loose chains flailed into the wheel arch taking great chunks out of the mudguard. By the time we had arrived the Wr.T. resembled something out of a stock car race; all battered.

The schoolgirl was still trapped underneath the bus's front wheel. Her schoolmates caused it, and the other would be passengers by pushing forwards as the bus arrived, thereby shoving her into the path of the bus. With the snow on the ground the driver had no chance of stopping in time. As the bus slithered to a stop it trapped the girl, by the toes of her left foot, under the nearside front wheel. The snow around the crushed foot was now bright red with the blood and tissues of the limb.

Two wheel chocks were placed under the rear wheels of the bus to stop it from rolling further forward. The driver, who was still in his seat, was asked to reverse away from the girl, but he was frozen to the spot with shock. Barry Woods tried to assist the driver out of his cab, but the driver's hands gripped firm the steering wheel. So Woody had to peel the drivers fingers back one at a time before he could help in out of his cab. Sub O. Jack Foden said, "If we all push and Barry releases the brake we might be able to free her."

All free firemen, in attendance at that incident, placed themselves in front of the Leyland Atlantean bus, whilst L.Fm. Ken Danks rendered first aid to the schoolgirl helped by Bernard Newbound. On Fodens command we pushed against the weight of the double decker, still full of passengers, up the gradient of High Street hill. At first we didn't think we were going to move it as we tried to overcome the thin layer of snow that let our feet slip and slide. Then suddenly the bus started to move up the slope of the hill, allowing Ken Danks to pull the girl free.

The crowd once more surged forward to see what had happened to the girl and, by doing so, blocked the way of the ambulance men and Ken carrying her to the ambulance. The next thing I knew Ken was passing the girl into my arms to place her in the ambulance. She lay their quietly and never cried at all. I looked at her foot and it was flat, void of its shape, with very little blood to be seen. Around the top of what was once her shoe there was a clear jelly like substance with traces of blood running through it. I placed her onto the stretcher bed and left her for the ambulance men to treat her injuries.

On returning to the station, and during the period of changing over the equipment onto the replacement Wr.T. (the original had been taken 'off the run' due to damage caused by the broken skid chain), Jack Foden wondered if we could have released her quicker by towing or jacking. We tried several methods but still we couldn't reduce the time it had taken us. The time was recorded, by the messages sent from the attendance time to the 'stop person released', as just 3 minutes. We even tried pushing the Wr.T., fully kitted out and weighing around ten tons, up a lesser slope and we couldn't budge it an inch. It was, therefore, surmised that it was the adrenaline running through our bodies that had enabled us to complete the task in the time we did.

Finding myself down at 'Rocko' for a week meant that I didn't need to keep packing and unpacking my kit. I had hoped I would be able to use my motorbike as transport for the week, but the snow had put paid to that. My being down there also meant I had to rise earlier to get to work on time, but three years of getting up at 0745 hours had spoilt me for having to get up thirty minutes earlier now to go to Division Street.

It was a surprise when on my second day, as I waited at the bus stop, John Horsley pulled up and offered me a lift in his car as he was going to 'Rocko' for an promotional interview at 0930 hours with the C.F.O. I thanked him and climbed into the car. As we drove along it became obvious why my bus was late; the snow on the Penistone Road had caused several minor accidents and these were blocking the road. Which affected the bus I should have caught by delaying it so much that it had not yet completed its outward-bound journey. John said I should get out at the next telephone kiosk and call the brigade to say we were held up and that we would be a little late. This I did, but his next remark took me aback.

"I should get out and walk to work," he said.
I said, "I would willingly get out of the car and walk to work under normal conditions, but with the pavements so bad and the distance I have to travel, it

was not on my planned itinerary. But if that's what you want I'll get out now and wait for my bus, which is also stuck in the traffic jam. I'll probably arrive about an hour after you get there."

I made my move to get out of the car but he finally saw my point of view. We were, in fact, only one minute late for my 0900-hour start, and I would still have been waiting for the city bus if it hadn't been for his kind offer of a lift.
The day shifts passed and I started my fourth shift on duty, on nights. These were fifteen-hour shifts, starting at 1800 hours and finishing at 0900 hours the following day.

'Rocko' was short of B.A. wearers at this time and I was sent down on detached duties (D/D) as several of its senior hands had caught a cold bug of some kind. It was a funny station to work at, or so it seemed to me. The men were very cliquish, but fortunately they befriended me, although not everybody was so lucky.

D.Bentley was one who didn't strike the right cordial note with the men he worked with, although he must take the blame for a large extent of the troubles that came his way. 'Rocko', at the time he was on Blue Watch, was made up of Ex Guardsmen who had either served in the Foot Battalions or the Household Cavalry. On his first night on duty, a shift on which I was also present, the men asked him if he had done any foot drills as some found it hard to do at first.

"Of course I have," he replied, "I've marched for the Queen."
Now that was to be either the making or breaking of this young man, depending on his answer to their next question.
"Which mob were you in then?" queried Barry.
"St. Mathias' School, when the Queen visited here after her Coronation in 1953 at Wednesday Football ground," replied Bentley.

Now a look of incredulity swept across the faces of the men standing around. Was this man taking the 'piss' or what? The answer he gave was true. He had marched for the Queen, but not in the manner they meant. Was his parading any the less valid than theirs for being guardsmen or his for being a schoolboy? Whatever you think, it was not the correct answer to welcome him into the brotherhood of ex-servicemen. As for them, they marked him down mentally as a prat; therefore, he was fair game for any practical jokes he would fall for.

The first one he fell for was age against youth. They bet him that the oldest member on the shift was faster and fitter than he was. He accepted the bet to prove them wrong.

Bernard Wass was fifty-one years old, but was still a fit looking man and he had the bearing of a soldier. It was decided that they should each run up the staircases at opposite ends of the appliance room until they reached the top floor, then descend by the use of the pole chute into the engine house, finishing at the Duty Manning Board. The Sub O. was roped in to start them off.

"On the command 'OFF', you both know what you've to do," said Jack.
"OFF," he shouted.
As the two men ran hell for leather to their respective staircases, he added, "And you lot can F...off if he gets hurt."
On reaching the staircase Bernard stopped and walked back into the engine house and over to the bottom of the pole chute, where he wrapped his arms around the pole as though he had just landed.

On hearing the bang as the pole chute doors were flung back, we all waited for Bentley to appear at the bottom of the chute. With a thud he hit the rubber matting, then, scrabbling to keep his balance, he raced Bernard to the board, just finishing a few feet behind him.
"See, I told you he's a lot fitter than you," said 'Rooster' Hollingworth, "he's hardly broken into a sweat and tha looks knackered."
"Yes, but I was only a couple of feet behind him," said Bentley.
"Do you think you could still beat him then?" asked Barry.
"Yes I do," was the reply.

So once more it was repeated and once more he failed. Bentley couldn't understand it. He claimed there were more stairs at his side so they changed over, but still he kept on failing. By now, Bentley was sweating profusely, whilst Bernard was as cool as a cucumber. Rooster finally let him in on Bernard's secret. Bernie didn't start to brake, when coming down the fifty-foot chute, until the half landing above the engine house, some eighteen feet.
"Great. I'll beat him this time," he said.

So once more the performance was repeated. We heard the crash of the pole chute doors and the slithering sound as his body came down the pole chute. Finally we heard him grasp the pole to slow him down. Thank God he slowed himself down enough, for on hitting the mat he crumpled into a heap. That was enough for the others and me; at this rate we were likely to kill him, so on picking him up and finding him OK, we said, "That's enough."

"No it isn't," remarked Bentley. "I nearly beat him down, didn't I?"

"Are you still interested then?" asked Barry.

"Certainly," replied Bentley.

Several of us though, had had enough. It wasn't funny anymore. So as Bentley hurled passed me on his way up to the top landing I grabbed him.

"They're having you on; you can never win," I said.

"Oh, but I'll practice on my own to beat him," he commented.

Even though I had told him, he was still under the impression that he could beat Bernard, so I left him to carry on practicing on his own at night. His training sessions came to an end when Reaney's wife complained to the boss that when we were on duty there was always a lot of banging about and using of the pole chute. Reaney's flat was directly opposite the dance floor/bunk room, pole chute door, so eventually an order was issued that the pole chute was out of bounds except for fires, and skiving, but that's another story.

One of the other anomalies retained from the days when all firemen lived on the station, was the 2300 hours parade for the final muster roll call before going upstairs to the bunkroom. It was thought at the time, expedient to make sure that the fireman on duty had not gone back home for whatever reason.

At 2250 hours we started to mingle around the appliances in anticipation of the parade, and as usual some had gathered to watch the night revellers going home through the windows. When Sub Officer Foden said, "we had better move away in case we had a repetition of something that happened a few months earlier."

A group consisting of Barry Woods, Jim Green and Jeff (Rooster) Hollingworth were eyeing up the women, returning home with their boyfriends after a night out. Just then, a large group emerged from the Foresters a public house opposite. Obviously they had been to a private party there. The women, on seeing the firemen standing near the doors, started to blow friendly kisses to them. The boyfriends took umbrage at their actions and started to call and make fun at the firemen. The people involved were mostly teenagers; many of the men were dressed in the latest 'Beatle' style of suits, whilst the women wore the mini skirt and boots. One bloke, much the worse for drink, came staggering over to the doors and started to shout abuse at the group standing there.

"F...ing tosspots," he slurred.

"Wanker!" mouthed Barry.

"Who you calling a wanker?" cried the man.

The two stared at each other through the glass windowed doors and what happened next must be put down to alcohol. In no normal circumstances would a sober man decide to pick a fight with the ex soldier facing him. All of a sudden the man threw a punch at Barry through the glass pane. Barry rode the punch and seizing on the man's predicament, knocked off the counter weight that caused the doors to fly open, dragging the man inside with his arm still caught up in the broken window. As the man came into range, Barry socked him so hard in the face that he immediately crumpled onto the floor. That was it. The men accompanying the prostrate man now swarmed into the station through the opened door, lashing out at any firemen who came into view. Barry's voice could be heard to shout, "We are being attacked," as he felled another man.

It was the control room attendants who put the 'bells down', but soon the duty men were joined by the off duty men as they fought in a melee. Arms, legs and fists were flying everywhere. In brief moments from dealing with one youth Foden saw Stn.O. Ginger Booth standing in the pole chute well, fighting off three youths. His stance was that of an old fist fighter and from the safety of the pole chute his fist came stabbing out like a claw of a hermit crab. Jim, on seeing his predicament, hurled himself at the youths surrounding Stn.O. Booth. At some time in the course of the fighting Foden was handed a pick helve and with swirling motions of this weapon and the occasional stab in the belly, he, along with the others similarly armed, drove out the drunks back into the street. By this time the Police had arrived and arrests were being made of those still fighting in the street. The women, seeing their boyfriends being arrested, started to jump on the arresting officers' backs to try and stop them being taken away. Eventually all was quiet, and a roll call was taken together with injuries noted. Of the twenty on duty at 1800 hours there were two missing, and these were returned to the station by the Police, with thanks to the two for saving a Police officer from getting any further injuries after he was set upon when apprehending a youth fighting in the street. The youth was alleged to have pulled out a knife, but none was ever found. Who were our two heroes? None other than Barry and Jim, two of the original group who were partially to blame for the fracas in the first place.

When questioned later it was discovered that the two were still fighting a group of youths about two hundred yards away from the station, but as they claimed, "We couldn't see a fellow member in blue being beaten up by a group of youths." The facts were never bottomed and only two youths actually appeared before the courts; the first who threw the punch at Barry and the other was the knife carrier.

What injuries the youths received we will never know, but our lot received two broken noses and several black eyes and split lips.

January 1968

We were once again to represent the station in the Brigade Quiz. Walt has taken on the job of getting us to the peak of perfection as far as this quiz is concerned. If we win this time it will be a hat trick for this Watch and station, a feat never before achieved.

The new Sub Officer Jeff Overton seems a very relaxed character and not one to be bullied by conventions. Although he does P.T. with us in the morning, under Arthur Unwin's instructions, he doesn't put all his heart into it like Walt. Arthur Unwin has added a new fitness regime to his P.T., that of five-a-side football. The only trouble is, half of our shift are no good at football, although Jack, Keith and Paul were excellent at it. Arthur Unwin, at one time, thought of swapping men around. This was so that he could have a station team that could play any time there was a match, but because of Walt, (bless his cotton socks), and the quiz, it was pointed out that station personnel are there to fight fires, not to play football. Jack was so impressed by Paul Parkinson goal keeping abilities he renamed him 'The Cat'.

Changes were once again being talked about and one of the topics was the taking over of the area bordering Sheffield from the West Riding, though what especially interested us was the taking over of the Shell-Mex Petrol Depot at Ecclesfield.

It was through these discussions that Arthur Unwin was ordered to take part in combined exercise at the Depot. His orders were to treat this exercise as an actual incident and not to dawdle as we normally did when working with the Riding lads, to let them get there first.

The day duly arrived for the exercise and we beat the Riding by several minutes and had got water on the tank drenching system by the time their first pump rolled up. The Riding Brigade as expected took the main work and their foam tender was put to work pumping foam onto the tank designated as being on fire. Right from the start it was a fiasco. The pump failed to produce any foam and an irate West Riding D.O. turned onto Arthur Unwin and said, "Well you wouldn't just stand around at a fire if this was happening. Do something."

Arthur Unwin was taken aback at the way he was spoken to. He had arranged for our pump to be in attendance, and it had achieved what it was told to achieve. Initially he'd been told that as long as he got there first and set the water drenchers to work his duties were finished. He was also instructed that he was to attend as an observer, so he had come in his undress uniform with his fire kit in his Volkswagen car. Arthur Unwin shouted to Jeff to get a No 2 F.M.B. branch to work from off an adjacent storage tank and direct the foam to work from there onto the tank involved.

This we did, and as we started to pour foam onto the offending tank, the Riding foam tender managed to get its No 10 and 20's to work. These produced large amounts of foam and to get there own back on us for beating them, they let the produce of one of these branches pour directly over us, drenching us in foam solution. Arthur Unwin thought this was hilarious, and when we started to withdraw, he ordered us to stand our ground. Our only course of action was to turn our foam branch in their direction, but it failed to reach them. We withdrew to another position, out of reach of their monitor, and waited until we had further orders to 'knock off and make up'.

All the while, Arthur Unwin laughed at our foam-coated uniforms. That was until we had finished the de-briefing. The Ridings D.O. bollocked us all for messing around on an exercise, he played hell with the foam tender crew for not going through the right sequence when delivering foam, although when challenged what the sequence was, he evaded the question saying, "It was up to them to know." He slagged Arthur Unwin for positioning men on top of a storage tank during fire-fighting operations, saying, "We might have been killed in a real incident."

Arthur Unwin retorted, "When this risk comes under our control, we will have a fire plan and equipment that will work."
The officer didn't like that remark and said, "my findings will be going to both sets of C.F.O,s along with comments from Shell-Mex's management who were watching."

After he dismissed us we started to load up our appliance with the dirty equipment we had used. Arthur Unwin, still smirking, gestured to us how clean he was and then, pinching his nose, he intimated that he was glad he

Training in High Eaxpansion foam. To get us used to its claustrophobic qualities - no sight or sound. Note: Guideline H.E.F used in basement fires etc

wasn't going back to the station with us, smelling of foam compound with its animal protein base.

Grabbing hold of his car door handle he pressed and opened the door catch. No sooner had he broken the door seal when gallons of foam compound came flowing out of his car all over the lower half of his legs and feet because he hadn't closed his window properly. We cracked out laughing at his misfortune and Jeff said, "Let's go now."With Ken driving we set off on our way back to the station. As we drove out of the gates we could hear Arthur Unwin shout for us to stop and swill out his car; but like Nelson, there are times to obey orders and times to ignore them, and this was a time for the latter.

By the time Arthur Unwin rolled back on station, we had cleaned ourselves off and started to clean off the appliance. We all stood and watched as he got out of his car. With great deliberation he moved out his soggy legs, then, followed by a sucking sound, he raised himself from the driver's seat. He moved very slowly as he squelched his way back to the office, from where we could hear him laughing at his own misfortune.

The Auxiliary Fire Service has been mothballed and one of the saddest sights was seeing the A.F.S. Station Officer and his wife come in and do a vehicle check prior to these appliances being withdrawn back to the Home Office garages where they will be stored for future needs.
Ever since I joined, this couple always checked off the A.F.S. appliances, whether they were going out to Chorley on exercises or not. Even over the Christmas period this married couple would do a vehicle check. It had amused us to see them; him in his battle dress and her in the standard fire mackintosh and trousers, they looked like something left over from the Second World War. He, in fact, had been a fighter pilot but hadn't seen much action as he served in South Africa. Jack and Bert uses to sing to them as the checked off the appliances. It would go something like this:

"Standpipe Key and Bar?"
"Yes, Colin."
"Standpipe?"
"Yes, luv."
"Hurricane lamp?"
"Yes, luv."
And all the while, Jack and Bert would be sat or stood nearby, arms on each others shoulders, singing:

"There'll be Bluebirds over,
"The white cliffs of Dover,
"Tomorrow just you wait and see."
But now Colin and his Mary were saying good-bye to the appliances they had served so long. Today there was no mocking singing, we felt sorry to see them go. I was also saddened for my own liking for this service was due to joining the AFS in 1963.

Our shift was not the only one to see changes. For a short while, whilst Cliff Dickens was on leave. White Watch had Sub Officer Bernard Rippon, up from Division Street. Bernard was now in his last year of service and looking forward to his retirement. This man had never been married and had all the outward appearances of a vicar, and, like many a parson, he had some eccentric habits. These came to my notice at the beginning of this month, when we had a snow shower that left a coating of snow for several days. The snow on the first morning looked great, as it always does before the populace turn it into slush or compacted ice. It was, therefore, a surprise for me to see Bernard Rippon cycling to work on a motorised bicycle, (the kind that had the engine in the rear wheel), dressed in brown shorts and long knitted wool stockings pulled up to his knees. His only concession to the cold was a long red muffler, which gave him the look of an aged schoolboy.

Thinking about it, that's just what he was, an overgrown schoolboy, for he lived with his sister, and between them their lives had altered little with the passing of time. As children they used to cycle together, and although their parents had died, leaving them the house they lived in, nothing had changed for them since their childhood. Since enjoyment was taken, as children, by cycling, they continued to cycle, although they had now bought a tandem since his sister found it increasingly difficult to pedal long distances. Perhaps they never married because each one thought the other needed them more. As children they were blissfully happy together and now, as middle age crept on, they were still happy together. Many would say that to be happy through your life was a great success, but I think they missed out on life's rich tapestry by not seeking a partner.

Such was my surprise that morning, seeing this red nosed, red kneed man struggling along the road, battling against the snow, that I remarked to him, "that's the trouble with those small bike engines, they're so unreliable."
"Oh no, my dear fellow, there is nothing wrong with the engine, I just feel that it is cheating to use it," said Bernard.
"So you mean to tell me you've rode all the way from town, some eight miles,

pushing against the snow and the bike's gearing?" I asked.

"Yes, quite so," he said, sticking out his small chest, "Marjorie and I don't like cheating at anything." And with that he walked off into the station to get ready for work.

It was around this time we had another a new Leading Fireman, Jim Wardle. Walt Dawes had been promoted to the new station at Rivelin as Sub officer and with him he had got Dick Ash as his Leading Fireman, but because the building isn't completed they are manning the station's appliance from Division Street, so it is quite crowded down there just now.

Out of the Varley/Dawes shift of eight men, five had been promoted leaving Jack, Smithy (transferred to Division Street), and me still has firemen. I believe the reason for the success of this shift was the fact that Varley and Dawes created good all round officers, plus the fact that for three years in succession we won the Colin Hill trophy for fire ground knowledge. We even represented the Brigade in a National Quiz at Derby. Despite this as Tom (who had been transferred back onto Red Watch) said, "don't rush to get promotion Arthur, get some service under your belt, learn from the fires."
It didn't satisfy me at the time when a Fire Brigade Committees member's nephew was promoted with has little as two years service.

Overton and Wardle soon had our new shift working as a team and I found Cawthorne, Binnington, myself classed as old hands. I was now the one Jeff and Jim relied on especially with Breathing Apparatus jobs, because Pete and Douglas were confined to driving the appliances. This miffed Doug because all the house fires occurred when he was driving. It was with this new shift just after Derek Walker had come onto it, we received a call to assist Rivelin.

At 1600 hours a little boy had fallen into the swollen River Rivelin as he was making his way back home from fishing. By the time the alarm was raised, the night sky had drawn is veil over the city, and the child's parents were grasping at straws in the hope that we would find the boy safe and well.

The river had risen four feet in the last 24 hours and many of the side banking, never submerged before, were now awash. Nobody knew exactly where the boy was at the time he had fallen into the water, but his fishing rods were discovered about a quarter of a mile beyond the new fire station at Rivelin. This area was one of the initial steel forging areas of the city, and in times past the river had powered the water wheels that drove the hammers that forged the steel. To keep the wheels turning several dams had been built to secure

59

water supplies in times of drought during the summer months. These dams were now full of fish, and the water wheels had long since become still. It was in one of these dammed areas that the young boy had fished; just above the start of the lower Don's many weirs.

Our crew was turned out to watch for the body floating past Malin Bridge before the river turned into the Owlerton area. There the river met up with the River Don and it was to this area that there were now serious threats of flooding. A line had been set up across the swollen river to try and arrest any large objects flowing down stream. Doug was the driver of the appliance and only he kept dry, as he had to listen to the radio for information about the incident, in the warmth of the cab. The rest of us spread out along the bridge wall to watch out for the body. It didn't take long for the rain to penetrate our fire-coats, even though they are supposed to withstand absorption for at least 24 hours. Large objects kept floating past, stopping momentarily as they snagged on the line stretched across the river, only to be torn free by the force of the water. A large 50-gallon oil drum came bouncing along the river; every now and then it would be dragged under by the current, only to emerge a little further away.

"God! He stands no chance in that flow," remarked Jeff.

"Keep your crew's eyes peeled, Sub," said D.O. Smith.

Our miner's lamps stabbed the darkness of the water for any signs of life, but after an hour some of the lamps were starting to dim. I turned mine down to the pilot bulb, in an effort to conserve what little power was left in the battery. To my left was 'Daffy' Walker, who marched up and down like a caged lion.

"How long are we to stay here sir?" he enquired of the passing D.O. Frank Smith

"I dunno. Until the Police find the body or call off the search so until then concentrate on looking for anything that resembles life," said Frank, walking away.

Smith had moved about fifty yards away when Daffy yelled, "There's something in the water. I think it's a collie"

Smith immediately turned on his heels and ran back to where Daffy stood pointing into the river. Frank was in his late fifties, over weight and had only two months service left to do before he retired.

"What can you see?" he puffed.

"Sorry sir, I thought I saw a cauli but I can see now, it's a cabbage," Daffy said straight faced.

Smith glared at him, but was too short of breath to shout. We stood by for most of the night, and by the early hours of the morning the Police called a halt to the

Malin Bridge from where the firemen had watched for the boy's body

The weir close to where the boy had fished where his body was located

vigil until daybreak. We left the scene knowing that the parents would be going through hell. The remarks made by Daffy were his way of coping with the strain.

We went back to the station for our supper before being turned out to the Wincobank valley area. The houses in the bottom of the valley, around Arthur Lee's steelworks, had started to take in water into their cellars. The water in most of the houses was only a few inches deep and Jeff told the occupiers that there wasn't enough water to get the ejector pumps to work. This information was repeated throughout the night as he assured the owners there was nothing he could do. The occupiers of the terraced houses that were on some part of a hill were instructed to call for the service again if the water level rose to within a foot below the electric boxes and fuses. He explained that the low-level pump needed several inches of water to work properly and that their house cellars would collect the water from all the others in the terrace through drainage, as was already happening. Occupiers placated by his explanation, we were now free to deal with the more urgent cases.

Jim's sense of humour also came out this night, and his love of the Goon Show. I think every lad, born around the time of The Goons in the 1950s, had his favourite character. For Jack Furniss and I it was Eccles, but Jim preferred Colonel Bloodknot or Little Min. To find somebody as daft as yourself is quite rewarding, but when you discover that there is a whole shift of barmpots makes you think that madness isn't so special. Such antics as Daffy, for instance who would run his hand through your hair, every time he passed you, and shout "Zingbanda", made you feel quite fretful for your sanity, but on cold wet nights such as this one, we needed to cheer ourselves up.

Another thing that came out on the night was the fact that Douglas had a lisp when he got excited, and as I have a stammer, this caused a lot of leg pulling. I also remember that Barry Jones, when he first came onto the shift, got very excited when talking and suddenly he started to stammer. Trying to ease his embarrassment, I told him of how I was accidentally kicked in the face at the age three. I continued my story by telling Barry how twelve years of speech therapy under a Miss Gray (who I had a crush on from the age of 12) taught me how to control and almost eliminate my stammer by anticipating conversations and by singing to strengthen my vocal chords.

"Ffffu-fu-ckkkking Army would have c-c-c-cuured you quicker. They'd have put you in the sssssssssignals like me," he stammered.
Needless to say, if the Army cured him, I was glad I didn't receive such

technical treatment.

Douglas was saying that he would have to go back to the station for his fuel, tank after a night of running around, was getting low.
"I thay Jeff, we will afther go back thoon asth the fuel isth low."
"I think you hath a point Doug, letsth go back to base," mocked Jeff
"There'th no need to take the pisth," snapped Douglas.

Yes, this shift has definitely changed from what it was a few weeks ago, but I doubt it will be the premier shift on the Brigade. I certainly think we will be the clowning shift of the Brigade.

A day later the river gave up the body of the little boy. He was only a few feet away from where his fishing rods were discovered. The force of the water had driven his body under the river banking and it had been held in place by his fishing basket. There was no joking when the body was discovered; we felt only failure for not discovering it sooner, even though there would have been little chance of reviving him.

Wardle was at again last night regaling us with tales of Pirbright Guards Depot interspersed with brigade stories. Although last night must go down has a classic. He started telling us of the night they had a call from West Street Royal Hospital. It appeared a man had arrived in casualty with a nut stuck on his penis.

So Sub Officer Alex Watson and crew were dispatched to the hospital.
"This is a delicate operation we are to attempt, and I would prefer it if we could limit those in the theatre to a minimum," said the doctor.
"We followed the doctor to a side theatre in the casualty department," said Jim. "Where there was a young man sat on a bed with his lower garments removed. Over his private parts was a towel."
"Why didn't you bring the rest of the Household Cavalry with you?" remarked the patient.

"Well sir, we thought you'd like some privacy," answered the doctor, "but seeing that you agree this will be of medical interest to all concerned. He paused..........Do you want to bring the rest of your crew in," asked the doctor turning to Alex.

Fortunately for the patient Alex was not one for shows. The doctor stood at the left-hand side of the bed, Alex and Jim opposite him at the bottom of the bed, while a few nurses, gathered in what space was left.

"Right Ladies and Gentlemen. What we have here is a delicate surgical problem," said the doctor. He lifted the towel to reveal the man's predicament'.

"We have tried placing ice packs to reduce the swelling of the penis, but as you can see it is still very swollen and causing the gentleman pain," continued the doctor, prodding his finger into the man's groin.

"You'd never believe such a small thing could create so much fuss," remarked the sister sarcastically.

"What I'd like you to do is saw it off," said the doctor.

The man had a look of fright when he thought that Jim was being asked to sever his manhood.

"I mean the nut of course," added the doctor.

"All right Jim, start sawing through with the junior hacksaw," said Alex.

"I had hoped you would have one of the power tools to do it," said the doctor.

"Sorry mate, but this is the only saw we have for this type of work," said Jim.

"Then I'll go and see to the other patients. I'll keep popping back to see how you are progressing. Sister here will guide you in the medical needs," he said smiling.

With that he left, and we started to saw away at the steel nut, the nurses keeping it cool by pouring water onto it. When Jim got tired of sawing he handed over to Alex, but after a short while he said, "This is no good bring him to the station."

The patient was glad to get rid of his audience of nurses but he was in for a real shock. For when he and a nurse arrived by ambulance at Rocko to his horror he discovered that the whole station was waiting to witness the man and nut freak. Alex soon got rid of unwanted guest by saying all that stood around would be asked to take turns in the sawing of the metal nut. Jim said he had no sooner finished talking and the hose room was clear of sight seeing fire service personnel. Alex grabbed the man by the nut and pulled him over to the vice where he secured it.

"Well mate, it's a stupid thing you did; fancy placing a left hand thread on a right hand prick," said Alex, he then paused adding, "you are right handed?"

"Yes," responded the patient without thinking.

"See, you can always tell a right from left by the way it rises to the occasion," chirped in Jim.

Alex continued to saw until the blade needed changing then I took over;

continued Jim, "trying not to touch or saw into his prick". Alex steadied the nut by tightening the vice against movement whilst I tried not to snag the saw blade too much, but occasionally this happened, as it had done as we sawed away. When it snagged it caused the man extreme pain. Now if he was a masochist then we were only adding to his pleasure, I told myself, but the tears in the man's eyes made me think he wasn't enjoying himself. A few older hands came back to see how far we had got, also to give a hand in the sawing. Wassy, and Clarke then started talking to the man.

"It's actually cocoNUT oil that's good for a sore prick."
"Does your girlfriend suffer from PMF (PRE METAL FATIGUE)?"
"When you found it was stuck did you bolt for the door?"
"Your prick doesn't need a thread on it to screw somebody."
"It's all right having sex with a woman but you can't beat the real thing."
"Does the hardware store ban you from handling the goods?"
But the best of all came from the patient, "I felt such a prick when it got stuck."
We all gathered he had been feeling a prick at some time.
The nut was only partially sawn through when the ice packs being applied by the nurse and Alex, finally worked enough to allow the swelling to be reduced for the nut to be slipped off.
"Do you want the nut so you won't make the same mistake in size again?" asked the nurse disdainfully.

May 1968

Ernest Daniels had been a copper for twenty-two years and now they too were being asked to change, but the old style Constable found it hard to accept the changes being thrown at them. Ernest loved to talk to people he met on his beat, and friendships had grown out of these conversations. As he patrolled the streets he could call in many a house and be welcomed. It was always his routine that when on our beat he would take his tea breaks with us, as did the lads from 'traffic' and horse patrols. All would find their way to the station in time for tea and toast. The horses knew that when they were near the fire station it was time for a fresh pail of water and a few crusts of bread. We didn't mind them coming, for it added to topics of discussion and to have another body's view on the subject. Even when on night patrol, it was many a Constable who sought out the Watchroom attendant to mash him a fresh brew of tea. These inter-service gatherings bonded us together, for no fireman would see a Policeman struggle without the offer of assistance. Looking back, it wasn't so long ago that firemen were drawn from the ranks of the Police. It was a cosy arrangement, when men in uniform were allowed to make decisions on how they achieved their goal.

It was a sunny spring morning and we had settled down for our tea break when Ernest popped his head around the door.

"Have I missed it?" asked Ernest, referring to the tea.

"No, sit thi sen down," said Elsie.

Ernest told us why he was a little late. He had a new Sergeant, and he was a stickler for making point checks on the Constables. "So," he said, "I'll have to be on my toes for the next few weeks."

He put his radio on the table and tucked into his break, retelling the latest incidents he had been to. He had got partway through telling us about the drunks fighting outside The Magnet Public House, and how he had to flatten one of the drunks who had taken a swing at him. "I caught him with a left hook," he had just said, when the bells went down for a road traffic accident.

As we moved to the appliance Ernest slowly made his way to the Watchroom, eating his toast as he went. Jeff appeared from the Watchroom and said, "R.T.A. on Paper Mill Road, persons trapped."

"Bloody hell," cried Ernest, "that's right at the other side of my beat to pedal."

"Ge'us an 'and," Jeff said, picking up Ernie's bicycle.

So Jim helped Jeff place the bike on top of the ladder and we all set off to the accident. Ernest was quite chuffed to be with us, especially since it was saving him having to pedal. The accident was on one of the side roads near to Ecclesfield.

On arriving, we got to work and secured the safety of the vehicle and us. Meanwhile, Ernest got his bike from the top of the appliance, and not a minute too soon, for his Sergeant arrived in a squad car.

"You got here pretty fast, PC Daniels," remarked the Sergeant.

"Daniels my name, and cycling my game," replied Ernest.

We, by this time, had disconnected the battery and run out the hose reel, while Jeff and Jim examined the casualties. There were two people injured, one in a small flat back pick-up truck and another lay by the roadside.

The accident occurred when the pedestrian stepped out from between two parked cars, straight into the path of the truck. The truck driver, trying to avoid hitting the man full on, swerved away out of his path yet he still gave him a glancing blow with the front wing of the truck. The result of his valiant but in vain action resulted in him driving into one of the many trees that lined the estate roads. When the truck struck the tree, the driver was impacted onto the steering wheel, causing him, we suspected, a broken pelvis.

The other man complained of pain in the lower part of his leg and slight pain in his side, when he was knocked back. We set about immobilising the injured limbs on both casualties. Jeff, having ascertained that the truck driver could be lifted out when the ambulance arrived, had treated his injuries where he was. I placed around his waist two broad bandages, tying them off on the uninjured side. We were confidently treating our casualties when the ambulance from the 'Ridings arrived.

Ernest had backed up our call, and also requested an ambulance, as was the procedure. Which service control gave the address to the ambulance operator I don't know, but because the accident occurred near the border of Sheffield and the West Ridings, we had got a new Ridings ambulance serving in Sheffield area.

So what did it matter that an ambulance came from 'the Ridings' instead of the City? Well the 'Ridings' had just bought a fleet of American style ambulances that could only take one stretcher passenger, and we needed the space for two, like the Daimler ambulances of the City. The ambulance personnel said, "Not to worry, one can sit in the front with the broken leg and the pelvic injury could lay inside being attended to by my mate."

This we did, carefully lifting the man off the grass verge and placing him in the passenger seat. That done, we went to the truck driver and for the umpteenth time he was told not to pass water. Having placed our casualties in the ambulance, we held up the traffic to let the ambulance proceed to the hospital in Sheffield.

Jeff went over the casualties' names and addresses with Ernest. Everything checked out correct, so we were now ready to go back to the station. Then we noticed that the Police Sergeant hadn't left the incident, something was worrying him. Ernest was just about to leave when his Sergeant came over to him.
"I left you fifteen minutes ago at Sheffield Lane Top, and I was heading in this direction when I was informed of the accident," then giving Ernest a quizzical look, continued, "and you still beat me here. How?"
Ernest shrugged his shoulders and as he pedalled off said, "All I did was pedal and ring the bell."
"I've got my eye on you, Daniels. I've got my eye on you," shouted the Sergeant.
Well, we thought, at least he is finding work for both his eyes.

Ernest never did finish telling us his tale, and because he had left so much unsaid and the remark about the left hook, we nicknamed him 'Lefty' from then on.

A little Postscript to this accident; later that day when Jeff was confirming injuries with the hospital it turned out that it was the driver who had a broken leg and the pedestrian had pelvic injuries. As Jeff commented the hospital must have got the names wrong. It couldn't be that we had been so wrong. Or could it?

Lefty didn't stop coming to the station, but within a few months the Sergeant was also a visitor to the station for the occasional break. Yet the most regular was Pc.Bill Pettigrew, who used to come to play Paul at chess on some evenings, and he liked to talk about his days in the army as much as our blokes do. So now we had bomb disposal added to our curriculum.

June 1968

Another working set down at Division Street, and as usual the relief men outnumber the station men when it comes to doing fatigues. By the time the special duty men have been dismissed to mend hose, service the BA's, extinguisher maintenance, map maintenance men and hydrant cleaners, there is only the relief firemen and a couple of others, (usually recruits), to do the work. On the first day we cleaned all the windows of Division Street, yet at Elm Lane this doesn't require you to slip and pitch the Ajax Ladder every time you do the window cleaning as it does down here. Mind you, the lads try and make the work interesting by playing practical jokes on the others, or the public.

The first prank they pulled was on one of the new Assistant Divisional Officers, Ron Weston, who secretly goes to watch the educational programmes, shown for schools or universities, on the morning TV? They let him settle down and get into a programme; then they put pins into the television aerial cable, and by so doing, disrupt the picture and reception. He would then stroll out of the TV room and complain that he could never understand why a building on such a high promontory, could never receive a picture. They used to do a similar stunt to the A.C.O., by sticking pins in the telephone cable and twist them about, in the hope that it would disrupt his conversations. Yet this came to an end when the GPO telephone engineer told him after he had complained to them after one such prank, "that the yobs from the pubs had been tampering with the cable and that they had severed several

68

Fm 251.A.E.Levick
Ceremonial Uniform

Photographed By
A.Holmes

Bedford water tender

Blue watch Elm Lane 1965:
Fm. T.R. Smith, Fm. A.Rosier,
Sub Varley, Fm. J. Furniss

Sub O. 140 Thomas William Varley, Elm Lane on
Pc. Ernest Daniel's bike

Janet and I married on the 26th July 1965. There were no raised crossed axe arch for us to walk beneath and very little in the bank. With a token honeymoon of two days it was back to work for both of us. For Janet it was Englands Shoe Shop and for me back to dry fire drills. With cries of marry in haste echoing in our ears, Our marriage stood the test of time, a partnership which was til death do us part.

Re-Union

On probation report added to qualities "This man can draw"
Paintings, below, Moorhead, Sheffield

of the wires", so he relayed it out of the way to avoid it happening again. Another one we pulled was on a Saturday afternoon. Barry and Tony went into the F.P. offices and borrowed the female and child mannequins. Taking them to the second floor ledge, we placed both models on the ledge, securing them with a rope. Tony meanwhile, went to his locker and put on his civvy clothes and waited until a group of people started to pass the station, he would then look up and start shouting, "go on ya silly bitch, jump."

This would immediately make people look up to see this woman, with a child in her arms, stood swaying on the ledge.

"I've told you before, that kid's not mine, so jump!" Tony would shout up.
People who had gathered would then start playing hell with Tony for the things he was saying. It was then time for us to appear with the old jumping sheet, that was now full of holes and torn, and position ourselves to one side of the suspected victim. The last time the jump sheet was used was back in the fifties, and since then it had been used to cover the oxygen compressor.

"If she jumps you'll miss her," someone would say, or,
"You can't let her jump into that moth-eaten thing."
"Are you going to jump?" Tony would shout. Then John Haigh or somebody would rock the dummy forward.
"Don't jump love," we would cry up to the woman.
The after gathering enough spectators we would say, "Oh well! If she's not going to jump we'll go in."
"You can't leave the lass like that," someone would say.
"Are you going to jump?" we would shout up, and, on getting no reply, we would shrug our shoulders and start to go in.

Tony would have slipped away by this time, and as soon as we started to go in, John would push the dummy off the ledge, giving his best imitation of a woman's scream. The crowd would look up and gasp as they saw this young woman and child come falling towards them, only to see the victims suddenly bounce back up on the end of a rope, back into the second floor window.

"Silly buggers," they'd chunter as they left.
I always thought that deep down they wanted her to jump in any case.
Variations of this stunt would be pulled during the following hours and occasionally it had to be terminated very quickly when an officer was on the prowl.

The other stunt, which accompanied it, was the fat wallet on a piece of string, which would be pulled back into the station under the doors by a fireman hiding behind one of the machines. This was best done at night with drunks. But one drunk outsmarted us; he put his foot on the wallet before we had time to drag it back. Such were the childish games we got up to that it was no wonder Lambert used to treat us like kids sometimes.

Dave Parkes was playing hide and seek from the L.Fm. and had hid, like we used to do, in the pole chute, wedging our bodies against the walls. This was an excellent skiving hole, for if anybody came near, you could grab hold of the pole and the next second you were away into the engine house before they could find you something to do.

Dave had been avoiding the L.Fm. all morning and was getting bored, so he decided he would give one of the station cooks a fright by jumping out in front of them as they past the pole chute doors. He heard footsteps approaching and just at the right moment, he jumped out and shouted 'BOO'. Unfortunately, it wasn't a cook, but C.F.O. Lambert. He looked dismayed at Dave's behavior; "You are coming for a promotional interview next week, FIREMAN Parkes."

Sure enough he didn't get the job for that or the other reason. He got himself so uptight over the interview that he fainted when he entered the Chief's Office. It would be many a year before he would be allowed to try again.

July 1968

Tony Spriggs finally over-stepped the mark when once again the devil made use of his idle hands. The lads had been doing the usual dummy routine and, when putting back the mannequins, Tony had kept the child's hand. Frequently on weekend's parents brought their children to look at the fire station. One such parent was standing at the station doors looking in through the windows, as Tony passed the child stuck out his tongue, so Tony shook out his sleeve and let the dummy's arm fall into his hand. By the deftness of his hands he produced the dummy hand and proceeded to poke the child dummy finger up his nose. The effect was not what Tony had expected, for by the appearance of a child's hand from a man, it looked like he had a deformed hand. This gave the child hysterics and in due course a letter of complaint landed on the Chief's desk. It was inevitable that our practical jokes were then suspended for the time being.

August 1968

I have started to take driving lessons and this has, once again, broke the bank, so I am wondering whether to sell my motorbike. This I am very reluctant to do, but it might come to it, depending on what wage rise we will get in November.

The driving lessons have been going well except for the occasional set back. Mick Grant has been my usual driving instructor, but today I had to have someone else. The man given the job was called Mr. Birchington. Some people you can strike up an immediate rapport with, but this was a man I found I could easily dislike. His mannerism for a start, got to me. He treats me as though it was he who was doing me a favour by letting me drive his car. You wouldn't think I was paying for its use.

"Now Mr. Levick, what do we do before we set off?" he asked.
"We check to see if we have got the ignition key," I joked, trying to break the ice.
"No, we check the mirror."
I could see this was going to be a joyous hour.
"Right," I said, "we check our mirror, if all is correct and clear, we signal, then manoeuvre."
"Correct, Mr. Levick."
I started to pull out into the traffic when he started to tug on my coat sleeve.
"Pull into the side." I did.
"You didn't look in your mirror," he said.
"Yes I did."
"No, Mr. Levick, you must move your head, like this," he made an exaggerated movement of his head, stretching his neck toward the interior mirror and back again.
"Oh, come on, if you drove like that, by the time you had gone half a mile you'd have cramp of the neck," I replied.
"The examiner will want to see head movement."
"Can't I talk him through what I am doing?" I suggested.
"Let's try again," he said.
Off we went, down the main Hillsborough Road.
"Pull over again, Mr. Levick," he requested, pulling on my sleeve once more.
Again, I pulled up.
"You are using the third gear."
"I know, I was doing over 20 miles per hour and this car seems to want you to change gear," I said.

71

"But I don't like pupils to use third gear until they have had four lessons," he responded.

"I've held a motor cycle licence for nearly ten years, and I think I know when an engine will allow you to change gear."

"Carry on Mr. Levick."

Once more we set off and had only travelled about a quarter of a mile, when he started to tug, yet again, at my sleeve.

"Your road position is correct."

I looked at him, waiting for him to add to his remark but he said only, "Carry on Mr. Levick."

We set off again, but every few minutes he kept stopping me by the now familiar tug on my sleeve. Halfway through this lesson he stopped me again. "You keep telling me you are checking your rear view mirror, but I don't see your head move," he commented.

"As well as telling you I have looked, I also tell what cars are behind and what other cars are doing in front, to show that I am looking for others."

"I like head movements," he said, tugging on my sleeve once more.

I stopped the car, turned off the engine and said, "You f---ing tug on my sleeve once more, I'll break your bleeding arm." With that I started up the car and headed back to the driving school. He sat there very quiet, but I could feel him pressing the brakes as we went along. On getting back, I stormed into the office and played hell with the owner, saying I wanted another driving instructor and another lesson, as I wasn't willing to pay for the last effort.

I got my usual driving instructor, the next time, and a free lesson.

When relating my driving lesson to the crew of Elm Lane, at tea break the following day, A.D.O. Reaney said he would put me down for a test with the fire engine when I had had twenty lessons. On completion of the number of lessons required I applied to Reaney for the test promised. He told me to report to Division Street on my second rota day and he would assess if I were up to taking a test. This I did, and found there were two of us to be assessed for driving. That day, Roger Gee and I, took it in turns to drive the light van. It was good for both of us for we had at least four hours driving.

Reaney said, "I'll test you Arthur, tomorrow, and you Roger, the following day". Boy, was I pleased when Reaney pulled up in the light van loaded up with extinguishers. I remembered that my instructor said, "A test only lasts for 20-30 minutes at the most." I was therefore confident that I could drive at least that without putting a foot wrong.

We started out, through and around Sheffield city centre, and Reaney said, "Whilst we are out, we will drop off these extinguishers at various city libraries."

No problem, I thought. We drove all over the city, and after about twenty minutes he said, "Stop here." He then told me, as we went down City Road hill, he would slap his clipboard on the dash and I was to make an emergency stop. We set off, and part way down the hill he did what he said, slapped the dashboard. I brought the van to an immediate halt, quite safely and under control.

"That's good, Arthur, you can see why we always secure things like these extinguishers now, can't you?" he said. After driving for an hour, I thought I had blown the test as I had expected it to finish after half an hour. Wrong again Levick; the test was over a full day's driving and three other types of vehicles as well. From Land Rovers to light vans, and a wireless car with its column gear change. The test lasted six hours, driving completely around Sheffield, before he started the question session.

"Well Arthur, you have passed, and it will be on orders that you are classed as a light van driver. I have to make the test longer than normal to make up for the fact that you know the examiner, but all in all, it is a fair test," he smiled. The test was fair and I felt great confidence that I could manage any vehicle they put me to drive. I was over the moon with joy when I told Janet, "Now I'll sell my bike and buy a car."

Roger Gee wasn't so lucky the following day. When told to do an emergency stop, coming down City Rd., a false spindle flew out of a faulty hydrant cleaning kit box and, as well as smashing the windscreen, it struck Reaney at the side of the head, causing him to require hospital treatment.

"I wanted to ask him if I had passed my test, but it didn't seem quite right," said Roger. A week later, Roger was passed out as a driver, examined by a head bandaged Reaney.

September 1968

I have passed my driving test none too soon, for we are to have a Rescue Tender stationed up here. The chief has contemplated putting a T.L. or an

73

H.P. up here, but since the Shell-Mex exercise, we have found out that British Petroleum are to take over the site, and for the time being everything is to remain status quo. The only building changes planned for the Ecclesfield Petroleum Complex is that the site are to pass further pipes from the railway discharge terminal, under the road, to the tanks, instead of the overhead pipework as it now stands.

It felt funny going out on my own to do hydrants, today. Before, I have accompanied Keith, Ken, or any other qualified driver, but now I have my licence, Unwin has decided that one man can do both duties with regard to the cleaning out and booking of the hydrants done. It has been mentioned to Arthur Unwin that the books will get into a right state because of the hydrant man, having just cleaned out a muddy pit, will then have to write his findings in the book. Another thing I'll miss is the company. As we went about the streets we would discuss station happenings and family life, with its myriad's of problems. You got to know your workmate better in the confessional box of a van cab, than you did when he was in the full company of the rest of the Watch.

All things taken into account, I loved working away from the eyes of gaffers. By now I had cultivated a great number of places to have a tea break, without going back to the station. This meant that those in charge had lost control of you as soon as you past through the doors of the station, and only by your return did they regain control. This often meant that they would put you back onto the appliance, whilst they skived off to do other duties. The sense of freedom that driving gave me was great, and it was to become my sanity saver in years that followed.

My regular port of call was to a cafe I had attended when in the company of Keith Parker. It was in this cafe that two young teenage girls approached us. For a lift to Manchester, they would be more than grateful. We played along with them until out tea break had finished. We couldn't believe they had approached two men in uniform, driving a bright red, fully marked pick-up truck, for a lift. How did they think we could explain our absence? I don't mind bending a rule, but that sort of trip would be hard to explain if you broke down, never mind the mileage you'd have to explain away, unless of course you disconnected the Speedo cable. At first we thought they were winding us up, but to this day I am convinced that we would have got our evil way with these ladies if so desired.

If not attending the cafe for breaks, I used to visit friends or relations, and even old girl friends. As I have written previously, we did about twenty hydrants, and the rest of the day was ours.

Another reason to be released from fire fighting duties was the servicing of public buildings' fire extinguishers and other extinguishing aids. The places you serviced most frequently were the local schools in your station area.

The discharging and recharging of soda-acid water extinguishers never caused a problem. You only had to be more careful when dealing with the old type of acid phial with its lead stopper. Sulphuric acid had an affinity for the water and over a period of time the water would dilute the acid in the phial. It was therefore necessary to keep a check that the content level in the phial hadn't raised too much. If it had, you would throw away the contents and replace them from a carboy of acid carried in the van, always remembering to give it a good flushing of water to help it disperse and dilute.

It was on one of these extinguisher maintenance jaunts, with Walt Dawes, that I was taught a good lesson about drainage of buildings. We had arrived at the school just after nine to get an early start. We had informed the school secretary we were on the premises as previously arranged. It was only a matter of finding a suitable sink with a water supply, and we would service them on site, rather than return to the station to discharge and recharge, as we often had to do when servicing the libraries equipment. This took up a great deal of time.

We went around all the classrooms whilst the kids were in assembly, and removed their classroom extinguisher and replace it with a fire service one. This usually took until the morning break. At this particular school we had struck up a friendship with a woodwork teacher. I don't know who used whom the most. He told the head teacher that he would supervise us whilst we used his craft room; this got him out of attending assembly, which he hated, and in grateful return he kept us supplied with tea and biscuits from his secret store. Seeing teachers from the other side of the work spectrum was a great eye opener. Kids think that it's only themselves who like to bunk off from lessons, but some days, teachers feel the same. This particular morning, we had a steady stream of teachers join us in none scheduled tea breaks, all part of Woody's tea club.

After eleven o'clock we had started to discharge the Foam type extinguishers. So to speed up the process it was usual for one to take the inner solution and pour it down the internal sink, whilst the other would take the outer solution and pour it down a drain as far away as possible. This practice had been carried on for years but the new St.Peters School brought it to an end. I had poured the last of the solution of 8% bicarbonate of soda, with its 3% of stabiliser, consisting of siponin or such dissolved in water, down a drain near the playing fields. As I walked back with the empty outers I could see foam starting to come up one of the playground grates. Hurrying back as fast as I could to the woodwork room I intended to tell Walt that the foam solution was mixing in the drain under the playground. I had no need to say anything, for as I entered the stock room in which we were working, I could see Walt's feet covered in foam. The sink he had been using had no 'U' bend or any other pipe fitted to the outlet. The water went straight from the sink into a hole in the floor. So the mixtures met, and the aluminium sulphate solution combined with the outer solution was producing vast quantities of foam. As the stock room slowly filled with foam, we frantically opened up the tap full blast to dilute the solution. Having eventually stopped the chemical reaction, we were left with a load of wood and science laboratory flasks filled with foam. Never have I worked so fast to hide what had happened.

We hid the wet, foam soaked wood by swapping for the dryer wood stored further off the ground. Then we washed out all flasks and test tubes that were contaminated with foam and restored them, before the next teacher came back for a quick drink. Although we were never 'rumbled', I often wondered if the foam soaked wood had any effect on the finished product the kids made. Also, why the hell was science equipment stored in a woodworking stockroom?

October 1968

Bernard Mansell the brigade electrician, better known to the firemen as 'Thirteen Amp', his apprentice was known as "Five Amp", has started to fit two-tone horns to the appliances as well as the bells. From now on we will be Dee-Derring to fires instead of Ding-Dinging. He has also started to rewire the Watchroom ready for the new Tannoy system that will be installed later on.

Thirteen Amp had finished the Watchroom and was busily adjusting the horn compressor on the Wr.T., as it had started to squeak rather than blast, when we received a fire call to attend a chimney fire. No thought was given to Mansell as we sped away from the station. Jeff tried the new horns, but they didn't work, so he reverted to the bells. Peter commented that he could hear a banging from somewhere, but with all the tackle we carried it was hard to pinpoint what was loose. On arrival at the incident we discovered our loose component, it was Thirteen Amp. We had forgotten he was there.

"Ya mad sods! Ya don't gi a chap a chance ta get off before ya set off," said a very windswept Mansell.

Everyone is eager for the new Watchroom system to be introduced, although there will be plenty of changes and reduction to Watch personnel. The thought of not having to do Watchroom duty is being welcomed by all, and men that never used to sleep when on Watchroom Duty, now get their heads down once the station is quiet. For myself, I shall keep a wakeful Watch, as the shock to the system when the bells go down is enough to give you a heart attack. And judging from the way some calls are entered in the logbook, it looks as though the attendant has suffered from a heart attack. The entry made immediately after the call, appears as though a spider has crawled across the page. The letters start off big and pointed and as their pulse slows down, it reverts to the operative's normal size handwriting.

December 1968

Out in the North Sea, a trawler was pulling in her nets. The crew were looking forward to bringing in a good catch of herring from Dogger Bank shoals. Nathan Moore was a fifth generation fisherman. He had served during the war on the minesweepers, and on his demob, went with his brother to buy their own boat. Over the following years the boat was paid for, but the large fishing companies proved too much competition for the small boats and Nat's brother packed in fishing altogether.

After the war men could earn a good living following the shoals of herring. The skyline on such an evening would be filled with the drifters and trawlers setting sail out of Lowestoft. Those days were now long gone, the greed of the fishermen and the big companies with their deep-water trawlers, had decimated the herring and cod fishing. Now, Iceland wanted to close their coastal waters to the British and others that sought her fishing reserves around her island.

Nathan's son had followed his father to sea, but wondered how long it would be before they too would have to haul themselves up onto the beach. As they hauled in their nets for the last time, it looked like their days at sea might be profitable if they could get this catch back to shore before the other boats docked, sending prices down to where good quality fish went into feeding cattle and pets.

Nathan hand operated the winch and for a moment looked at the cable hauling in the net as it wound on the drum. The catch was aboard and only the heavy steel weights, which kept the nets down, were left to be heaved aboard. It was during this operation that the steel hawser snapped, just missing Nathan's son and another crewmember, but unfortunately is caused Nathan to be knocked back. Nathan felt numb. There was no feeling in his body, only cold.

An R.A.F. helicopter from Leconfield was dispatched to the stricken trawler men, and within hours he was back on dry land having medical treatment. The doctors decided that if Nat was to be saved from being bound to a wheelchair, he needed the specialist treatment from the spinal unit at Sheffield.

We were turned out at 1758 hours to light up the landing pad in readiness for the 'chopper'. On top of Shirecliffe hill the winter night air blew straight through you, and chilled your bones. Shirecliffe Heliport had only opened in July of this year and we had hoped it would bring us extra work through "standing by" when helicopters landed, but so far it hadn't. On its opening we had all the top brass to oversee the touch down of the Westland helicopter from the R.A.F. This was followed by the V.I.P.s being taken for a short flight over Sheffield.

The pilot asked us if we wanted to have a go, but A.D.O. Reaney who, by the way, made sure he had a trip rejected the offer, on our behalf. We had to settle for a technical tour of the aircraft and the requirements the crew need to land the thing, which was all very enlightening, but we all wished we could have had a trip in one all the same.

Just after 1800 hours we heard the chopper's engine in the night sky. Eyes were peeled for any sight of the aircraft, but the low cloud made it difficult to see. Then the noise of the engine started to fade away as he overshot the landing sight. The Police and ambulance were ready to take Nathan Moore to the Lodge Moor Hospital. Radio co-ordination with the R.A.F. Air Traffic Control was done via the Police radio system.

Once more we heard the noise of the Wessex coming closer, and then fading away as he past over. The radio operator tried to tell him when he was overhead, but the pilot couldn't make out the landing pad.

"Right lads," shouted Unwin, "get every lamp and vehicle light directed onto

78

the pad. Arthur, get the searchlight to work and see if you can give him a beam so that he can pinpoint where he's to land.

The searchlights on fire appliances aren't used very often, and we had travelled over some rough ground to get here; so when Jeff shouted for me to illuminate the light as the Wessex made another pass, as soon as the light was switched on, it extinguished itself almost as quick. On examination I found that the glass bulb had become detached from its metal fitting. Typical! The only time we had ever required the light to throw up a decent beam of light, it failed. Fortunately, there had been a break in the clouds and the pilot could see the illuminated pad.

After Nat had been transferred to the ambulance, we had to await the return of the RAF nurse after handing over her patient to the hospital doctors. It transpired that the pilot had once previously brought a patient to Sheffield City General Hospital, before the spinal unit had been transferred to the Lodge Moor. So it was to that hospital and the fields adjacent to it that he was looking for his landing. What also surprised us was his navigation map. I'd always thought the R.A.F. would issue their pilots with the best maps, not the Shell road map he had.

He said he had followed the river to Rotherham, and then tried to find the motorway into Sheffield. Where was the fine precision navigation we are shown in war films? It reminded me of one of the tales the ex-servicemen told when they had retreated from Belgium to Dunkirk during the last war. The officers were given maps for the advance across Belgium, but not for the retreat into France. The maps for the retreat landed just as the last of the soldiers were being evacuated off the beach. The officers, who had purchased maps of France, requested reimbursement back in England but were told, "No chance!" Just like our helicopter pilot with his road map.

Several days later when Nathan's son visited his father in hospital, we received a box of cod from him, which was shared out amongst the men and the station mess. Nathan was never to return to sea as captain of his own boat and, I believe, his son also retired as a trawlerman soon after.

Event of 1968

The year began with a group of typists 'Backing Britain' when unemployment started to rise

Twice racing car champion, Jim Clark, was killed when his racing car hit a tree at the Hockenheim circuit in Germany
Then there was Enoch Powell's river of blood speech over the rising flood of immigrants into our country.

We had the start of two tier postal deliveries, and a first class comedian, Tony Hancock, committed suicide whilst in Australia.

Sixty trawler men died during the month of February 1968 off the coast of Iceland.

The main story, to the firemen, was the collapse of the twenty-two storey Ronan Point Flats, caused by a gas explosion, after which all Sheffield's flats were to have gas withdrawn from them.

Chapter 4

1969-1972

Officers and Gentlemen

They say you should never fall out with a colleague and it was good job we had remained on good terms with John Horseley because he was back up here as our relief Sub officer.

An ammonia tanker had been redirected from his last port of call to drop his remaining load at Tinsley Steelworks. He had planned his route out at the start of the day, but because of this alteration of his run he once more consulted his A to Z road guide. From the point where he was now, according to this guide, he could go more or less straight across by using the road to Fife Street and right under the bridge, which the book said would lead him onto the main Rotherham and Tinsley road.

He still had plenty of time and, with his altered dropping arrangements, he would be finished even sooner than expected; which was no bad thing. The traffic was light and the progress he was making was good. As he approached the Railway Bridge he noticed the sign warning all lorries to approach through the central portion, he checked his mirrors and signalled to take up the centre of the carriageway as he went through the arch. Just as he approached the arch a delivery van was doing the same, but from the opposite side of the bridge. Neither driver thought that the other wouldn't make way for him, but as they got nearer it was obvious that they were going to crash. Each driver pulled over to his own side of the carriageway and by so doing, avoided collision. The delivery van passed through the arch safely, but the ammonia tanker struck one of the supporting beams, knocking off the valve of his pressurised load. Ammonia now shot out and hit the bridge, under pressure, as a liquid, but before too long it vapourised into a gas excluding the oxygen about.

The driver grabbed his emergency breathing apparatus, which consisted of a bottle of compressed air with oral/nasal mask and pressed it hard against his face. Turning on the air cylinder he took several deep breaths before fleeing from his vehicle. For an area of 50 yards all around the tanker other drivers abandoned their vehicles as the invisible gas cloud encapsulated them. The

tanker driver, on reaching a spot where others were gasping but breathing without aid, took his apparatus away from his face. We had been quite busy whilst John had been up here and to give him his due he had been a good Sub Officer to follow. No one doubted John's ability and his calm way of dealing with what had been thrown at him during his full tour with us left us with a feeling that we wouldn't mind him being in charge again.

This latest incident more than confirmed our opinion of him and of how dangerous ammonia can be. On our arrival it was soon apparent were the gas cloud lay for it was like walking into a invisible wall, one minute you could breath the next you were choking. All I could think about was that it attacked sweaty parts and I tried to keep cool and calm though the running out length of hose and dragging it toward the tanker to form a protective spray, wasn't exactly cool work. Jack and Cappy Kendrick put on the new Normalair compressed BA sets only to find out, as gasped Jack Furniss,

"These don't keep out the ammonia."
John decided to use a series of water sprays to stop the gas cloud spreading, for ammonia has an affinity with water. The jets and sprays were spectacularly successful, which gave John a chance to have a think about the problem that faced him. The ammonia cloud had brought a halt to all the road traffic heading for Rotherham; it had also halted the main line rail traffic and shut down a block of offices opposite.

"It will take about half an hour before the relief tanker is available to take off the rest of my load," said the driver, "but I am willing to try and drive it to an open space - if there is one around here."

John thought a moment then asked the traffic Police if they would go ahead and see if the lay-by was free for the tanker to use. The patrolman nodded then he and his mate went to see or clear the lay-by for the tanker to blow off its load in relative safety. When this was sorted John said to me:
"I'll leave the Darnall crew to follow the tanker, you Arthur can carry on with swilling down the Railway Bridge. Whilst Jack and Ken provide covering sprays on the tanker until he is free. "

Once more the tanker driver donned his small BA set and getting back into his cab, started up the lorry's engine. At first it was thought that he wasn't going to be able to move as the tanker appeared to be jammed, but hesitantly and slowly the vehicle edged forward, giving off masses of sparks as the tanker rubbed against the metalwork of the bridge until it was finally clear. The

Fife Street, cleaning up ammonia spill;
Fm. K. Kendrick, Fm. J. Furniss, Fm. A. Levick & Sub O. J. Horseley

tanker driver followed the instructions given to him by John and the small convoy of vehicles set off for the lay-by.

Once the road was clear I set about swilling down the bridge. Even now in places were pockets of ammonia that made you gasp for air, but I carried on working and when such obstacles were met I withdrew to a safer spot where I could breathe. The one thing about ammonia is that there is no choice of - I'll stick it out until the gas thins - if it's in such thick concentration near you, you have to move.

I was quite happy doing my little task and Jack and Ken had finished theirs when the Star reporter turned up with a photographer.

"Can I take a picture of your lads working," asked the photographer trying his hardest to breathe normally.

"There is only him up there doing owt and he's nearly finished looking at the state of shit coming off the bridge," replied John.

So it was our fire crew and the photographer joined me on the bridge.

"Can you join him," asked the photographer of Ken who came to back me up."

"Arthur come here. Jack, go and back Ken up," said John.

"What's up," I enquired.

"Nothing, only Jack and Ken are better looking than you."

That why in the picture, they are looking as though they're interested in what's going on and I am looking straight at the cameraman. Like the little boy who saw the King without his clothing. Yet Jack should have been awarded an Oscar for his performance of a man working hard to control a jet.

This next section of my story revolves around a Station Officer who on the whole was so disliked I would find it hard not to cause him and his surviving family hurt. I therefore shall only refer to him as X. To be fair to him he would see his actions in a completely different light, and he would be able to prove he was liked by some.

Changes of personnel were a regular occurrence has you've gathered from this book. So when free thinking leader Unwin retired and was replaced with the autocratic officer in the shape of Mr.X, our joking and laughing came to an abrupt end. Although some things still amused me. I saw a bloke on the bus today and he had pulled the little hair he had over from his right ear to nearly his left, which made his head look like an egg covered with a three pieces of straw.

It was sad to see the lengths some blokes go to keep their hair. I myself have started to lose my hair of late, but I can do nothing to stop the retreat; in fact if it keeps falling out at its present rate I shall soon make a billiard ball look positively hairy. I have heard all the bald headed jokes, so I get them all in first to disarm any potential jokers and piss takers. Like: 'It saves me money - I don't have to buy a crash helmet I just paint a strap on my chin', or, 'I admired Friar Tuck so much I copied his hair style.' Yet that poor ol' chap is fighting a losing battle with nature and his hormones; if Prince Philip can't find anything to make his hair grow, then nobody can.

The funniest I've heard was from Mr.X. - I hate to say - but when he discovered I was growing a moustache to break up my face line, he said, "Why cultivate on your top lip what grows in profusion around your arse." But a bald headed man does need a moustache, for when you wash your face it's a guideline for somewhere to stop.

I was late this morning as Janet was ill again during the night and I was awake for the majority of it looking after my little love's needs. It was 1000 hours when I rolled into work and I expected a bollocking, but not to be put on a charge for absenteeism. This is the first time I've been late in nearly ten years and it makes me mad that I was on report for the first offence. To make things worse I've told Janet to ring me if she gets any worse, but Jim has informed me that the officers are under instruction not to let me make or receive any telephone calls.

It was my misfortune to be sent on short notice relief duties to Rocko' at 1100 hours; now if Janet wanted me she wouldn't be able to find me without a lot of difficulty. That day I was on tenterhooks as to Janet's condition and when I arrived home from work I found her on the settee, still suffering from head pains. I looked after Alan and tried to do what I could for Janet, but at about 0430 hours I had to rush out to get a doctor to her.

On his arrival he said that he thought Janet should go into hospital for exploratory tests. He couldn't, or wouldn't give me any idea of what he thought was wrong with Janet, only that it was in relation to great fluctuations in her blood pressure since Alan's birth. In the days that followed I put in a request to alter my Rota Day to suit Janet's day hospitalisation so that I could look after Alan. It never crossed my mind that my request would be or had been denied. So the day she went into hospital I went to the station to confirm I was all right to swap my day, only to be told my request had been denied and that I should make other arrangements for the care of my son.

"Your duty's here and if you are not at this station at the correct time, charges will be made," said Mr.X.

I went home and tried to arrange for either of the mothers to help me out, but at such short notice it made it hard for them to help out, although both said they would lose a day's pay to have Alan for me. It was Janet's mother who came up trumps. For Joyce had managed to arrange to swap her days for her to look after Alan until my mother finished her shift at the hospital.

Janet was kept in the dark about the arrangements I had made, as I knew it would have upset her as it did me. My anger at my impotence to look after my own child and for a set of officers who didn't care a toss about the welfare of their men.

Janet came home the following day and I was able, with the help of both mothers, to give her several days' rest - as prescribed by the doctor. The results of the test carried out on Janet proved negative and it would be in later life that Janet would find out the true reason for her illness. The next two months our time was taken up by hospital visits and medical treatment, which had limited success, but for the sake of Janet's health we were advised not to have any more children or place Janet under any stressful situation. During those months Mr.X. made my life hell, blocking and objecting to as many of my requests as possible. The final straw came when Janet rang me up to say that we were being sued over some work we had cancelled. I needed to get to use the phone but I was denied access.
I asked Jeff, " Can I use the phone for an urgent domestic call?"
Jeff shook his head and said, " He'll not let you."
"Whether you like it or not, if I can't use the station phone then I will go to the nearest public box and make any calls I have too from there."
As I walked out of the station I put all thoughts of further charges being brought against me from my head.
The next day I prepared to defend myself, only to be told that Mr.X. hadn't placed me on any charges and that I would not be facing any disciplinary hearing, now or in the future, with regard to these matters. Jeff said that he'd warned that he submit a report saying that I had been a victim of Mr. X's abuse of authority.

I was told to let things lie as they were and not to make a fuss about the way I'd been treated. This I did, but resolved to have my revenge on Mr.X. And from now on I would pay him back in anyway I could. Around this time I was having difficulty with Mr. X. a moral boosting fire occurred in the East-end of

Sheffield, to relieve the tension on station.

The day had been the usual round of drill and fatigues and I was looking forward to getting home and putting my feet up. My kit was clean and my boots polished for the next day's activities - whatever they be - when we received a Blue Spot call to a make-up with Darnall and Rocko'. As soon as we turned out we thought it must be a big incident as the radio traffic was so heavy we had reached the halfway point to our destination before acceptance of our mobilising message. Going down Barnsley Road we could see a pall of smoke rising from the general direction of Sheffield. The call was to a Firth Brown's heavy machine shop, which was under refitting and maintenance.

Two workmen discovered and reported the fire after returning from a short break. The fire was caused by hot droplets of molten metal falling from oxy acetylene burners used during the burning away of metalwork onto waste rags and paper that had accumulated during the course of refurbishment.

Slowly but surely it gained hold, burning down by the side of the stanchion, catching hold of the material lining the metal sheets cladding the building. Try as they may on their return to find the gable end alight, that attacking the fire with buckets of water they couldn't hold it from spreading. The fire was spreading externally as well as internally as the tar covered sheeting caught fire along with the fibreboard-lining sheet. This was always a dilemma for the officer in charge of the first appliance arriving, for he would often see the external fire risk before he knew about the internal one. Also when an appliance arrives at such an incident, he doesn't have the resources at his disposal to tackle either fire effectively. Such a dilemma faced the appliances from Darnall as the tar-covered sheeting was spreading the fire at a greater speed than the internal fibreboard was. By the time the O.I.C. became aware of the internal fire and he had resources to fight both, some twenty minutes would have elapsed.

When we arrived, the fire had got a firm hold of one end of the building and smoke filled the street between the steel complex. In the latter half of the sixties all the major steel manufacturers carried out a great building and expansion programme for it seemed the steel boom would go on forever, but in the seventies great cracks had started to appear in this hypothesis.

Firth Brown's were as guilty as the next in this belief for they had partially rebuilt and converted two machine workshops of over 400 ft on either side of Carlisle Street. The position of the buildings and the lay of the land now

Firth Brown Fire

Sub O. D. Griffen(behind) Fm. T. Perkins   Fm. T.R. Smith   Fm. M.Hurst

Firh Brown Fire, below heat damage to steel girders

FIREMEN at work amid the dense smoke.

Star picture from Firth Brown fire

Six years later, building could not be saved

91

trapped the products of incomplete combustion into a small confined area. The Heavy Machine Shop originally housed the great lathes used for machining gun barrels and other precision castings. Now, in this building soundproofing and lagging reduced noise and heating costs for the benefit of the environment and company profits. The building still had its tar covered sheeting and it was this that the officer first attending could see burning merrily away and giving off smoke.

Sub Officer of Darnall's appliance Keith Battersby I believe had tried to stop the spread of the fire along the length of the building by placing stop jets at the Sheffield side of the building near the junction of Carlisle Street and Saville Street. This temporarily stopped the fire spreading, but other forces were conspiring against him. By the time he had got to the entrance of the shop and walked back inside to the opposite end he discovered he had a similar fire burning on the inside as well as the outside. The internal fire had, by now, spread to a paint store temporarily set up for the decorators to use and this in turn had started to involve the acetylene gas pipe that relayed all around the works, for the gas welders and burners to draw off as needed.

A major fire was now developing inside the works with his resources committed to fighting a fire on the external walls. Without radio communication of today to rely on he now had to retrace his journey the length of the building to get back to his appliance and all the time precious minutes were ticking away for a fire, like time and tide, waits for no man. He decided to split part of his initial force to possibly make an attempt to hold the internal fire, whilst men on the outside had no comprehension of his reason for reducing the effectiveness of holding the outer fire. Some thought he had gone mad, but on getting inside the building and being met by a roaring fire, soon changed their minds.

At times like these an officer hasn't time to explain why he makes a decision and that's why a fireman always has to obey orders he doesn't really understand. We firemen attending this fire were to obey many orders without knowing the reasons behind them.

On our arrival at the incident instruction was given to get out pump into the Emergency Water Tank (E.W.T.) that was a legacy left over from the Second World War, when Sheffield was suffering, like many cities, from bombing. These Fire Tanks now served a similar purpose in peacetime; to supply water for fire fighting when hydrants were unreliable to give a regular supply. The Sub Officers didn't have to worry about the street main being bombed now, but he did have to worry that each fire fighting jet had enough water so that it didn't overdraw its supply, and this is where the Fire Tank came into its own. We set our pump into the tank and supplied Darnall's appliance with a fresh supply of water, whereby it could continue to feed the four jets it had out from its pump, initially fed from street fire hydrants. On completion of this task we were to run a line of hose out and find a wicket gate in the side of the building, where we were to set in a stop jet to protect the Carlisle Street side of the premises. Furthermore if possible to stop fire spreading over the roof. The smoke was now so thick in the street; we had to feel our way along the pavement, extending the line of hose as we progressed. It was a short time after entering the smoke cloud that I felt my helmet start to reduce in weight on my head and, looking at the floor, I noticed all the street rubbish heading towards the fire. Even at that point it didn't dawn on me what was happening, then suddenly Jim's helmet lifted off his head and started to roll away down the street.

"God! What's involved?" Jim said after regaining his helmet.
We slowly progressed until we reached the wicket gate. As we got nearer we could see two firemen from Rocko' crouched below a small flight of steps that led into the works.
"We've got the one inch nozzle", Barry Woods said.

We looked at one another bemused; what was he on about? It appeared that their instructions were the same as ours and he assumed we were just bringing the hose for their branch. After a brief discussion in our little area free from smoke, crouched below the steps, Barry pointed out that the acetylene main had eventually burnt through an oxygen main pipe that also ran adjacent to it. This created a mini firestorm inside the works, even after shut off of the acetylene supply the firestorm raged, fed by the oxygen.

After sending back the order for water on, the jet finally burst into life. Because of its one-inch nozzle it took four of us to hold it, and as there were six of us we decided to relief spell one another. This plan didn't last for long as officers kept coming around and taking a fireman away for other duties until eventually I was on my own to try and control this powerful jet. Now on drill there are at least two of you to hold a jet of this size, but as I've said many times before, 'fires are not like drill sessions'. So I was left to manage the best I could, fighting the jet reaction of the branch and the vacuum caused by the firestorm. It was a weird feeling, having your tunic trying to lift itself from your body and the helmet bobbling about on the top of your head, only stopping with you because you were biting the chinstrap.

I was in this position for an hour and I can assure you I was thoroughly knackered by the time two relief's came. I was fortunate in a way because the oxygen main kept the area surrounding me, virtually smoke free, whereas on the outside it was as black as night. The T.T.L. branch man had to wear B.A. to enable him to breathe in the dense cloud of smoke that was his working environment. Added to this; he had the fright of his life when Terry Smith had to move the T.L., with Perkins still aloft and the ladder extended to three quarters of its height. The fire at that point was moving so fast that by the time a stop jet was in place the fire had passed it, so Smithy had to relocate the ladder pretty smartish, under A.D.O. Ron Weston instructions.

Leading Fireman Terry Perkin, up top at the time, said, "I wasn't worried; I always wear brown underpants in any case."

The fire, like all major incidents, was one where the firemen start to obey one instruction only to have it countermanded by another senior officer, then, when the initiating officer came back to find his orders not complied with, he would bollock the fireman for not obeying the order. This happened to several members of our crew and Doug and Peter had their orders changed so many times, they put down their branch and went elsewhere for orders.

The fire, although contained before completely gutting the building, caused damage sufficient to require restructure, with different material used to clad and line its walls. Although the fire involved three quarters of the building, by carefully positioning the branches, we were able to stop any columns from buckling under the heat generated from both internal and external cladding. It was anticipated that the works would be operational within a short time, as none of the machinery was on site when the fire occurred.

(Six years later this same building was involved in fire, but this time the brigade couldn't save it. The heat generated by the fire caused the metal column to buckle and collapse.)

Having made up all the equipment we had used, or taken off the appliance by other fire crews, we set off back to the station, after five hours of fire fighting feeling satisfied that we had done our best. Mr.X. sat in the O.I.C. set and never spoke at all, which was unusual for after a big fire they either thanked you or castigated you for your actions. I wondered what it would take to please this man; we had all worked hard and, from his point of view he couldn't go wrong, it wasn't his fire so any mistakes made wouldn't be directed at him. I had noticed in the past how he would let Jeff make the initial decision then play hell with him and us for doing the wrong thing by carrying out Jeff's orders. Today he could decry the decisions made at the fire with total immunity - which should have pleased him - but ol' sourpuss sat and stared ahead. It was not until we got into the station that he opened his mouth. "Before you all dash off home, make sure that there isn't any mucky kit on the pegs."

It was a pointless thing to say, for after any large incident you inevitably needed to let your kit dry off before you could clean it. As we carried our wet gear to the drying room I caught sight of his kit, back on the pegs, unbuttoned, and his boots muddy.

Typical, I thought, then I noticed, as his car sped away from the station, he never looked to see if anything was coming along his side of the carriageway. My first thought was that he was a mad driver, as he could not see any of the traffic on the road until he moved from his parking space to the station forecourt. Then I saw Jim come walking across the road with the evening paper he had just purchased from Hebdidge's newsagents. What I believe Mr.X. did was, look to see if Jim or any other fireman was waiting to cross the road at the time he was preparing to leave; as they started to cross the road he knew that it was safe for him to move off. This thought was in my mind all the way home.

For the next few days I watched how and whom he trusted to walk across the road. He only moved off when it was Jim, Jeff or Doug who crossed never when Brian or Peter fetched the papers. I waited patiently for the moment to spring a little surprise on Mr.X., but I didn't have to wait too long. Jim was giving me a lift home and he mentioned that he would get his evening paper before he set off for home. I told him not to bother; I would fetch it for him and he could start his car engine and warm it up; by the time I had collected the paper he would be ready to set off home.

I noticed Mr.X., sat in his car, watching as I waited to cross the road, then, judging the moment, I picked out a car that was coming along and I sauntered into the road. I reckoned I could just make the half way stage before the car would be upon me. Each step I took aimed to show the onlooker that I had plenty of time to spare - Mr.X. took the bait. He set off from his parking space like a bat out of hell, accelerating all the way. When he cleared the wall obstructing his view he saw the car parallel to himself. I don't know who was the most surprised, Mr.X. or the other motorist. Mr.X. braked hard and I could hear his brakes squealing as he tried to stop the car before it hit the far side, station boundary wall.

God punishes man; and it seemed that God was on his side. The car came to a halt about one inch from the wall - he was lucky he had the station forecourt to brake on. When I came out of the newsagents, Mr.X. sat slumped, hugging his steering wheel. Jim told me what had gone off, but I think I could have guessed.

It was open warfare on Mr.X. from then on, for I personally thought we had taken enough from this man and I knew I wasn't the only one to bear a grudge against him.

Two stories emerged around this time one

First concerning Brian Marsden and Keith Riley our new replacement fireman and recruit, shortly afterwards, ran foul of this man. Keith used to pick up Brian on his way into work from Barnsley, where he lived. This particular evening Mr.X. had arranged a short notice relief for both of them at Rocko'. Although we didn't get paid for arriving early we were expected to be fully available, fifteen minutes before our shift start time. Over the last year, men had been questioning this ruling, especially since our pay rises were always the bare minimum, so an attitude was growing amongst the men that they would be there for the time from which they received pay. Keith and Brian rolled into work with ample time to get changed for parade, but not enough time for them to be on parade down at Rocko', as Mr.X. had promised.

"What time do you call this?" Mr.X. shouted at the pair.

"Well I make it 1750 hours, Mr.X.," said Keith.

"Don't f...ing try being smart arsed with me," answered Mr.X., as he pushed Brian toward Keith. "You're late!"

"No sir, we are early," came back Keith.

Mr.X. was fuming. He told them they were required at Rocko' for relief duties at 1800 hours.

"That's not our fault; we wasn't informed that we were going or we would have been here earlier," said Keith calmly.

The attitude Keith adopted was the correct one, for Mr.X. was completely in the wrong and was losing his temper as the minutes ticked away. Neither Brian nor Keith dawdled about, but every few steps Mr.X. pushed and harried them towards the van.

"I'll drive you down," snapped Mr.X. as he pushed Brian into the back of the van.

As they drove away we couldn't help feeling sorry for the pair having to put up with his mumbling all the way to town and yet within a minute or two we had forgotten the incident and got on with our evening work routine.

Their came a telephone call around 1830 hours saying where were the relief firemen. This was followed a short while afterwards that they had arrived. From this incident a story grew that Keith snatched the keys from the ignition and told Mr. X. he wasn't in a fit state to drive, and wouldn't give him back the keys until he had calmed down. Great as the story goes it wasn't true. Mr.X. had drove erratically and it had crossed the mind of those accompanying him that they should like him to calm his temper and slow down.

Yet such stories as this accompanied the man all throughout his service although each might be exaggerated. There I believe there was a strong element of truth.

Jeff asked them if they wanted to put in a report about Mr.X., as he had been completely out of order in his actions of the previous night.

A long discussion took place and decision made that it should remain as it was, as Lambert would always back his officers no matter how wrong they were; also it could lead to further victimisation as both were still recruits with nine months yet to do, of their probationary period.

Other things came out that night such as the way Mr.X. had slagged off Janet for bringing apple pies for our after dinner sweet. The new cook had refused to make them until she got the hang of the new, smaller cooker, and as I was running the mess at the time I had asked Janet to help us out. Mr.X., along with the rest of us, benefited from her good deed, yet one morning, because I had forgotten to bring the pie to work, Janet walked to the station with it and Mr.X. said to Jeff, "What's that c--t want?"

Had I known sooner about this remark, Janet would have stopped making the pies a lot sooner than she did.

Towards the early seventies our station was to get a further appliance, which meant an increase in Watch personnel. Who in our case turned out to be another ex-guardsman Malcolm Holland. If he were anything like his brother Mick who also served on the brigade he would make one hell of a fireman.

To Doug's delight the appliance designated is to be a Rescue Tender, which will mean that I shall be driving as much as he.

Friendly Faces

Mr.X. is in his element; he has two F.P. officers stationed up here until the new fire station is built alongside of this one. Why is he so happy? Well, they are his equals in rank and it allows him to make our life hell and still have someone talk to. Mind you, the two officers sent up here are not the most cheerful of men. After one inspection the Matron of Wharncliffe Hospital, when querying the rights of these men to insist that a piano be moved out of one of the wards used as a rehabilitation room, described that as being the "Rat featured and the Skeleton who did the inspection." It was from this description that they were then known as Rat and Skeleton.

Mr.X. now came down with all the venom he could muster; sniping at everybody. The first day of this tour of duty he was on about Brian and myself mucking up the roller towel in the gents' toilet and saying that we were a set of scruffs for not washing our hands properly before wiping them on the towel. Brian and I had just returned from the smoke house and he automatically accused us of this petty infringement, so we showed him our hands were still black from the job we had been doing, but he only muttered, "It's blokes like you that do it."

Consequently, when one morning I knew he had used the cook's toilet, I told him "I am refusing to clean that toilet as the last person who used it must have had a diffuser branch up his or her arse." A little later he was back in the toilet, cleaning up his mess, for although toilet cleaning is part and parcel of daily station cleaning, the female cook's toilet is out of bounds, even for officers' use, other than for cleaning.

These petty antics now make up our day, getting your own back in whatever way you can. In July, when the tomatoes in the station greenhouse first cropped, Mr.X. forbade that firemen are sold any of them, they were to be sold only to senior officers; who duly bought them because they were cheaper than in the shops. By the time of mid-summer the price in the shops went down and the officers started buying their tomatoes elsewhere; it was then that Mr.X. told us we could now buy the station grown tomatoes. The majority of us said, "Stuff them," and left them to rot in the greenhouse. If we couldn't have them when they were cheap, we certainly were not going to have them now they were slightly dearer than shop prices.

It was unbelievable that grown men should behave with such pettiness, but we wanted to strike back at this man in any and every way we could. When you were on days with this man he would follow you around, checking and re-checking every movement you made. He especially liked to hound Brian and Keith, so I taught them a hiding place or two where they could say they were working, but they would be free from his prying eyes. The best one, I told them, was when doing the daily lamp checks, go into the top of the tower and sit where the large extractor fan was, from there it was possible to see

Mr.X. coming and he couldn't prove how long you had been there. It was from this eerie that many of us sat and watched him circumnavigate the station searching for us, without ever being found out.

If he did one good thing, it was to bring all the firemen together against him. Mr.X. presence hangs over this station like a black cloud, yet when he's gone home or on leave it is like a great weight has been lifted from your shoulder. Mr.X. may have had many good qualities but his leadership methods were something to experience. If I learnt anything from this man it was not man management. A good officer is approachable, and he should be able to give and accept orders or advice, more than that he should have the men's confidence and respect. All which have to be earned.

Lambert started a private study period for firemen who want to study to pass their promotion examinations. A time was agreed and with the union's blessing it was implemented. Mr.X. called this, 'a charter for scroungers'; so once more he put up his objections as to why he wouldn't implement the system on his station.

For a while now Janet had been on at me to start studying for my promotion exams and this seemed an opportune time to start. Along with Douglas we got stuck into the studying; even Peter picked up a manual. This was fine, but Mr.X. didn't like us studying so he started a kit check to follow every study period. Now I've always had my kit properly marked up, but one or two never did. It was these men that Mr.X. would get at and through their idleness would complain to those that studied to give it up so that he would forget about the kit checks. One by one he wore the men down to forget studying; all except Douglas and me.

The Chief wanted firemen to go out to do basic F.P. inspections, especially the Office, Shops and Railway premises, and both Douglas and I were keen to do this. Although some didn't like the idea, to us it was a step in the right direction, it meant we had a better argument for pay rises and also we would be out of Mr.X.'s eyes; I thought every man would like that - the recruits did.
We kept on studying throughout this period of petty reprisals from Mr.X. until one day he came in and picked up the Home Office Training Manual on the O.S.R. Act, and said that firemen were too dirty to use such a book. That was it. I'd had enough. I rang the Union Secretary as this stations representative and told him, " I wanted clarification on just what the Chief wanted."

The response and reply was swift. Within 24 hours Mr.X. was on is way to Rocko' for a meeting with the Chief. No one knows what was said, but the outcome was that he gave us back the book he had confiscated and studying was, from then on, free from harassment.

The morning paper arrived and I was reading it when the Skeleton walked in and demanded I hand over the paper for an officer to read. His hands tried to snatch the paper from me, but my grip on it was too tight. He stood there, tugging at the paper, so I looked up at him and said, "Which window would you like to go through?"

Just then a friendly voice said, "Arthur, give me a hand with these smoke canisters I've brought up."

It was Walt; he had come up with a load of equipment to restock the smokehouse. He looked at me as if to say: let him have it, it's not worth arguing over. I released my grip and let Skeleton take the paper.
Outside at the van, Walt said, "Do you know what name you've acquired? Johnny Red! They blame you for every trouble that you take to the Chief."
"I only take men's grievances; I don't make them up," I replied.
"Last month you spoke up for certain officers wanting extra time to do fire reports," he said, "and the Chief doesn't blame those who told you to ask; he blames you. He even called you a liar when he asked you for the names," continued Walt.
"That was because I refused to name them."
"Do yourself a favour; let them fight their own battles. Stop firing bullets for somebody else," advised Walt and continued to unload the van.
"Where have you got all this information from?" I asked.
"It gets around; believe me, it gets around," he smiled.

At home, I told Janet what Walt had said. "Perhaps he's got a point," she said. For the next few weeks I thought much on what Walt had said, and when nobody turned up for the Branch meeting that was to discuss what action we should take if we didn't get a decent pay rise, I resigned from doing the union job. I bet they now wish they had turned up for that union meeting, as the Tories have put a wage freeze in force as from the sixth of November, our pay rise would have come into force on the seventh. The Police Force has already had their pay rise.

Officers and other Plebs

One of the new Sub Officers is the most conceited man I've ever met. Fred Tingle was promoted a few years ago and right from the word go he strutted about saying, "I will be Chief somewhere before I am forty."

Tingle was not aggressive, but by God he had got one hell of a mouth on him. One evening he walked onto the station brandishing a wallet jam packed with pound notes.

"I've made my first million today," he told his Watch.
"So you've had a good day then?" asked Brian Wilde
"I have laid the foundation for a fortune in a shrewd investment," replied Fred.
"Are you going to let us in on it?" asked Dave Egan.
"Luv to, but this is top drawer stuff," he said, shrugging his shoulders. "I've had to lay it on the line with these guys that no others dip in to spoil the kitty."
"Shame that," said Brian, snatching his wallet, "but you'll buy the lads a drink."
"Certainly, anything they like," he drawled.
With that, Brian dashed out of the station to the off-licence across the road and bought each man a bottle of his favourite alcoholic beverage. Loaded up with bottles as he was, anybody seeing him would have thought there was going to be one heck of a drinking spree that night.
Tingle didn't say much when Wilde gave him back a very depleted wallet, but continued to fantasize about this mythical money he was going to make. The trouble with Tingle was he couldn't differentiate between fact and fiction - he was a storyteller - and in medieval times he would have been a minstrel, telling stories of how he slew dragons. One night, in the office whilst waiting for the change over, we had the tale of how he had got rid of his high-powered boat so that he could buy a Helicopter. His house was close to mine, so he said, but I never could pick out this house with a searchlight illuminating the front walls. I had in mind a place like Disneyland, with towers and banners streaming from flagpoles on the battlements. The saddest thing is how he treats his wife, for she was lied to on an even greater scale than we were. Tingle had a great talking line when it came to women and he well and truly played the field.

Yes, this loud mouth was now being promoted to Station Officer and it was a strong possibility he might even talk his way to the top, for lacking in self-confidence this man certainly was not. He even held a celebration party every time he sat an examination, so convinced was he that he had passed. It was inevitable he would pass at sometime, and now he had we were all to hear about his meteoric rise to power.

"I'll never forget my friends," he said on the last time we met at shift change over.

Having to move house was the only drawback to this mans promotion and I finally discovered where he lived; it was just eight houses away and the searchlight was a small set of spotlights fitting into the rockery.

The Last Straw

They were burning off the derelict houses around the Wincobank Estate. I was driving the R.T. and Jeff had been told that Mr.X. might go to some fires today so he was to be prepared to take the first turn. This was awkward for both Jeff and myself for I didn't know when or if I had a passenger or not.

It was a call to the derelict houses that brought matters to a head. The horns 'went down' and Jeff picked up the message for the call's address. He now stood waiting to see if Mr.X. was coming or not. Mr.X. came to the door and rubbed his chin, then went back into his office.

"What's that supposed to mean?" Jeff asked. "Oh f...k him; I'm off!"
Jeff climbed into the Wr.L., told Douglas the address of the incident and instructed him to drive off. Under normal conditions I would have driven out immediately behind the machine and tagged along until we got to our destination, but I waited a few more seconds until Douglas was nearly out of sight. Still Mr.X. hadn't come out to the R.T. and I took it that he wasn't going to attend, so I started off after the appliance. I had got onto the main road when I heard a bang at the rear of the Land Rover. I looked into the rear view mirror and could see nothing so I kept on driving after the machine. WALLOP---! Another bang. I wondered if somebody hadn't fastened down the bank of Dry Powder fire extinguishers that the vehicle carried. Then, in the rear view mirror, I saw the reason for the noise - it was Mr.X., chasing after the R.T., throwing his boots at the vehicle to catch my attention, which he did. I pulled up and Mr.X. crawled in - an out of breath wreck. He didn't say anything at first, just pointed for me to go after the Water Ladder.

By this time Douglas was out of my sight and having no radio on the vehicle I had no idea of the address. My only hope of finding them was to follow the water trail left from the overflow of the tender. We were lucky it was a dry day and within minutes I had caught site of him once more; not that the Land Rover was fast, but he must have been caught up in traffic as some point.

The fire involved was a complete row of terraces in which the demolition men were going to work the next day. Because they are not allowed to take the wood off the site, sometimes to save time, after all the salvageable goods have been removed from the houses, they miraculously caught fire. The contractors claimed that when they left the premises there were no fires and so the children were blamed. In this particular case the children must have had a birthday for a whole row of six houses were burning.

These were well and truly alight, with flames coming out of every window and opening that the building had. The recruits used to like these types of fires because it was always a jet job. Even the older end, in whose numbers I now counted myself, didn't find them uninteresting, for it gave you a good idea how fire spreads through property and also lets you witness the collapse of buildings without any loss to the occupier. It was the danger from these fired buildings that you had to beware of and the rank had to keep an eye open for recruits who were always to the fore in this type of fire fighting.

When the Darnall appliance attended the incident it was decided between Mr.X. and Darnall's Sub Officer that because the whole row was involved the fire be split into two, we (Elm Lane) would take the top houses and they the bottom of the row.

Jeff ordered me to go with Malc, get another line out and start to tackle the next house in our section of fire. After charging the line we moved up the passageway between the houses and started to tackle the house we had been assigned to extinguish. The demolition men had dropped the floors out of several houses, to aid the burning, and the one adjacent to us was such a house. Malc was instructed by Jeff to be the number one on the branch, this was to give him some branch holding practice as well as to let him play.
As I have said, you could learn a lot from a fired derelict. By playing a jet on a wall you could swill out the crumbling mortar and cause it to collapse, or by playing direct at a wall or door you could knock it down or open as you had a will. Also you could watch with safety the collapse of a roof and how dangerous loose slates could be, also how you always needed to be vigilant that your water supply wasn't cut off by falling debris, for there was your life line back to safety. Another thing you could see was how other materials

reacted when burning; the green flame when copper is involved, the different aromas given off by substances that helped you to tell what was burning, even if you couldn't see it. Wood and coal for example have very different burning smells, yet basically they are the same stuff. Burning clothing and mattresses also have their own aroma and it was little things like this that could be learned.

I was telling Malc how you could tell this building was fired deliberately. There was no reaction from the electric wiring when you hit it with water; there was no molten lead coming off from where the flashing should be, despite how well alight the roof was; and had he noticed the smell of petrol when we first came to extinguish this particular fire.

"Stop f...ing yakking, we've work to do." said Mr.X., as he walked out of one of the derelicts. He examined the house we had almost put out.
"Come with me and do this one now," dragging Malc by the sleeve. As he moved off I noticed that he was going into a different house to the one he had just walked through.
"Not that way, Malc," I shouted. "Floor's gone in that one."
"I've just walked through it. Freetened o' a bit a smoke?" sneered Mr.X..
He set off to walk through the smoke filled derelict house and Malc made to follow him, so I grabbed hold of his fire coat.
"There's no floors in that one, I'm telling you," I repeated to Malc.
"Come on with that jet," bellowed Mr.X. with anger in his voice, the turned and saw me holding Malc.
"If you think it's that safe; you lead the way," I suggested, still holding Malc.
Again God smiled on Mr.X., for the smoke momentarily cleared when the timber in the cellar flamed up to reveal a ten-foot drop, two steps from where he was walking.
Mr.X. came out and left us to find our own way; he also left us to finish extinguishing the fires at the rear of the premises, as Jeff had wanted us to do in the first place.
"Would you have let him fall?" asked Malc.
"Well, I wouldn't have made him fall would I - gravity would," I replied.

Getting back to the station we found out why Mr.X. had taken too long to join the R.T. earlier. His blood circulation problem was affecting his walking again, but still he wouldn't go off sick. He hobbled around the station with two walking sticks made from cut down broom handles. These sticks, as he shuffled about the station, would occasionally slip on the polished, painted floor, causing him to slip and twist and bringing him severe pain, yet nobody said a word of comfort to him.

This has got to be one of the best Christmases I've known, even though I was on nights for the most of it. Janet told Alan to wait until I got home before he opened his Christmas presents, this was routine which the lad had to get use too, as she wanted me to witness the joy when he opened his presents. There were many things I missed out on in bringing up Alan, but Christmas was a family time and she always waited for us all to be together before any present was untied. Nothing could ever replace that moment; and they will stay in my mind forever, Janet's too.

Postscript Mr. X.
 After writing how bad this man was; if it wasn't for his report on me, recommending promotion, my career in the Fire Service would have come to nothing. Also several firemen including Mick Turner would always say Mr.X was true and loyal to his friends.

Events of 1969-72

1969
  Concorde 002 makes its first supersonic maiden flight.
  British troops are deployed in Ulster to control riots
  Kray twins jailed for life.
  Beatles stop performing live.
1970
  In January 2,850 die from "Hong Kong Flu."
  Edward Heath wins general election for conservatives.
  BP strikes oil in North Sea.
1971
  Rolls Royce car manufacturers goes bust.
  Postal Workers strike for first time.
  Margaret Thatcher ends free school milk
  Ibrox Park, Rangers Football Club, saw the death of sixty-six people
  when crowd barriers collapsed.
1972
  Coal miners call a national strike, government plans to ration coal.
  Bloody Sunday when two civil rights marchers are shot dead by
  Troops.
  Ted Heath signs up Britain to join EEC
  Idi Amin expels Uganda's Asians from the country.

Chapter 5

1973

Some are chosen

Work has started on the new fire station and the footings are being excavated. A man from the local history unit came to see Mr.X and asked, "What is going to happen to the old flitch gate at the rear of the smoke house and the old copper birch tree that the old coachmen used as a landmark to guide them into Sheffield?"

Well, I guess they will do nothing to protect either, but it is pointless talking to Mr.X because he will not do anything about it.
The other day, Colin (ex A.F.S. Stn.O.) came into the station to ask Mr.X to tell the lads that his father had passed away in his sleep. Colin's father was as well known to us, as was Colin himself, for he used to walk his dog by the station every morning at about 1000 hours. There it would refresh itself when the lads let it drink the water from out of the hose reel, or any other branch they were using.

On telling Mr.X about his death, Mr.X just shrugged his shoulders, and said, "What can I do about it?"
Colin turned, walked away and never returned to the station. As he walked away, his shoulders slumped, I thought, Mr.X you are the biggest Bastard I've ever met.

Station personnel transfers have come through and Jack has agreed to swap places with me and go to Rocko' in my stead; this, because this arrangement satisfies both our needs.

Jack to getaway from Mr.X, and my reluctance to drop my living standards; to where I would have had to borrow money to stop in the job. I therefore approached Lambert and told him I would be seeking work employment elsewhere if this transfer were to go ahead, so Lambert said, " If I could get a man to exchange with me, it would be all right by me".
The newcomer to the shift will be Barry Woods, who has been transferred out here temporarily as a mild punishment for one or two pranks he and Tony Spriggs have got up to of late.

The first bit of bother they got up to was caused by the new set up at Rocko'. The officers have got a section of the dining room all to themselves, as they always had, but now they have had the tables arranged so that it resembles the seating arrangements of Jesus' Last Supper. With their tables along the top of the dining room they seat themselves, in rank order from the centre position, with the Chief in Jesus' place and his disciples on either side. Those below the rank of Assistant Divisional Officer, that is the Station Officers, are on the wings of the set up. They can move up accordingly if a senior rank is missing. This caused a lot of mirth amongst the firemen, who aren't bothered how they sit or where, as long as there is a meal for them. The officers now also have created a problem for themselves, for they look upon the length of the table to see who is of the least rank there. For it is expected of him to play 'mother' in the pouring out of tea from their special tea service, together with the passing of condiments.

Another duty to be befall this lesser mortal, which has turned into a silent grouse. After serving everybody seated from the tureens the food remaining for them is cold. This led to a further problem that became evident with the tureen wallahs was when one of the A.D.O,s, one Friday dinner time, swapped all the pieces of fish for the tail ends of cod. When the firemen were having their dinner it was noticed none of them had a tail end, so they chivvied the mess manager to find out where all the end pieces had gone.
Again it was a petty gripe, just like ours with Mr.X. Taken in single context they amounted to nothing, but over a period of time the collective effect can be explosive.

The following Friday the officer repeated his action of swapping the fish, but this time Barry and Tony were watching him. They let him complete his task then, to get their own back, they placed one side of the tureens over the gas burner, leaving their side off. When the officers returned to collect the tureens from Tony and Barry, who were on mess duties, he presumed that because the two mess men had been able to pick up their tureens without a cloth for protection, they would be able to do likewise. The officers had gone only one or two steps away from the serving hatch when all the tureens went up in the air, spilling their contents onto the floor. I am told there was a lot of swearing going on and much waving about of hands, as officers tried to cool them down.

There was no more complaining about cold food tureens, no more picking which portion they had, no more special seating arrangements. The tables were returned to small groups albeit away from the firemen.

Because of their actions both firemen were transferred out, Barry to our station and Tony to Rivelin.

Mr.X spent a few days assessing his new acquisition and found him not of his liking for Barry being an ex-guardsman like himself, could play as rough as the next.

The tales of Pirbright grew. First Malc, and the time he went to Aden and his part of the army's task to win over the natives. To achieve this aim they opened up a Red Cross Post that was to serve the Arab populace with free medicine. As soon as it was opened there was a queue a mile long. Along with the many who were really ill came hundreds with splinters in fingers or minor complaints. These minor ailments were directed across to the orderlies and soldiers to finish treating.

"It was obvious, that many of them had come to get something for nothing," said Malc. Adding when asked, " where was the pain?" they would go into a great dance about pains in the head, so we gave them aspirin at first, but we couldn't make them understand what the tablets were diagnosed for or for which complaint. So the medic had an idea and said, " to stick the repeat tablet over the affected part of the body with a sticky plaster and to give them some in the hand."

"Great, we thought, but several days later these same Arabs were walking around with the tablet stuck to their head. From then on we stuck a tablet on the head of everybody we treated and they thought it was great! Barry followed on with his tale of how, when on U.N. duties in Cyprus after General Grivas EOKA terrorists had started their bombing campaign, they would ride through the villages in their armoured cars and if they saw anybody on the streets, they would bend their long radio aerial over and lash them with it as they passed.

If these are true examples of how peacekeeping duties were carried out, it's no wonder the world is in such a mess. Jim would bring them back to their peacekeeping role by talking about who was at Buckingham Palace, and did they still use the rifle butting signals to warn the gate sentries when the Royals were approaching. Was it four for Margaret and six for Her Majesty and a foot up the arse for the Royal Corgis?

May 1973
Keith, my brother, has resigned from the Police Force and is going to start up

as a Private Investigator. Over the last few years he too had become disillusioned with the way his career was progressing. Some of the blame must be laid at his own door, for he doesn't like to study for examinations and also he hasn't had the support from his superiors that he ought.

Supt.Smith said, "Over the last ten years the drug trafficking in this city has increased by 300%." Although the actual numbers were relatively small compared to the population of Sheffield, there was a definite increase in the use of illegal narcotics. This started around the mid to late sixties and revolved around the music clubs of that time.

Keith became more aware of this fact whilst still in the uniform branch of the Police. He arrested a youth that had stolen a car from one of the new municipal car parks earlier that night. Keith was on motorcycle patrol, doing the rural area of his division that took in a local Remand Centre and Hospital. Both organisations required a place outside the city and free from populace and pollution. The place chosen to site these premises was on one of the main roads that led away from Sheffield and towards one of our busy nearby airports. The E Type Jaguar, reported stolen, would have stood out from other vehicles at any time, but was even more noticeable by the erratic way it was being driven into Sheffield.

"Normally, when you got on the end of the tail pipe of a Jaguar, the first thing that happened was that the driver would try to lose you, but this joker just wandered around the middle of the road," said Keith. "I eventually managed to make him pull over and his manner and looks gave me the impression he was high on something or other, so I questioned him further."

(On later medical findings it was discovered that he was high on amphetamine-based drugs)

Another surprise to Keith was that he was so willing to be helpful and everything about him, under different circumstances, would have had you believing he owned the car. What transpired from their conversation was that a club he had attended required transport to the airport for a group of artists that had appeared that evening.
"Anthony volunteered to take the pop group over to the airport for nothing," it was stated by the club owners.
Keith didn't totally buy into that explanation. Furthermore on checking into the youth's background only to discover the annoying fact that he was so confident he wouldn't pay for his crime because of his father. Who had in the

past bought off various organisations so that his son never faced prosecution. There was also a strong case for believing that the private music club was being used to promote drug taking in the city. (We were in fact used one New Year's Eve to front a suspected drug dealing activities by the Police who used our powers of entry to search a private music club for such trafficking.)

When he produced his findings to his Superintendent, the case was immediately taken over by the C.I.D. to finish the investigation. Without so much as a word of thanks for the spadework he had put in he was brushed to one side.

There are many similarities in our jobs, I think.

Postscript

Eventually the lad's father had had enough, and from one his escapades finally had him facing a judge and was sentenced to a prison sentence where he was found to be a drug user as well as a supplier.

June 1973

We have been to a house fire in the remotest part of our area. It took us forty-three minutes to get to it. This was because there were no roads to get to this isolated cottage, only a rough cart track that was over grown in places. Mr.X instructed us to carry the equipment on foot whilst he and Jeff would go ahead in the Land Rover to see if they could do anything with the equipment of the R.T. With Jim in charge we loaded up the Ajax Ladder with equipment we might need; this was then lashed to the L.W. pump that had been placed on its carrying wheels. Once fully loaded we set off to follow Mr.X and Jeff whilst Peter tried his best to bring the appliance after us.

By the time we reached the fire it was nearly extinguished. Only little hot spots left here and there, which were soon dowsed. The cottage, we were eventually told, hadn't been occupied since a forest worker had left some ten months ago.

Peter finally got the appliance to us and we were relieved we didn't have to carry the equipment back. Out joy was to be short lived, for on our return down the track it was apparent that the path couldn't stand this heavy traffic. In our crew at that time we had a tank recovery expert and three others who had done vehicle recovery whilst serving with the Guards, as well as Mr.X. This being so, a problem like a ten ton truck should have given us no problem, you would have thought. Wrong again!

Mr.X.'s first command made sense - to drop the tank of water by letting it run out through a length of hose, away from the track. This we did, but the appliance had now sunk into the path where it stood. Jeff said, "Let the R.T. go around it and, by using its winches and the Tirfor hand operated winch we can do a two way pull, freeing the vehicle as well as moving it forward."

Mr.X would have none of it; "If it came in by driving it will go out by driving." He instructed three of us to cut down some saplings and place them under the wheels. The three of us; Keith Riley, Brian and myself, started to chop down the saplings while Jeff, Malc, and Jim went into a huddle as to what should be done. I saw Jeff climb into the R.T. to drive and position it in from of the machine. The others went and got the Tirfor set up to pull it back onto the path, which now was crumbling away under the weight. Jeff started to give Peter some instructions, but with Mr.X. bawling and shouting and Jeff giving instruction, it was little wonder that they failed to achieve what they set out to. "I f...ing told you; I'm in charge and you'll do as I say," barked Mr.X.

That was it. He had lost any useful input that the others could give, now it was being left to the civilian three, plus the driver and Mr.X, to get the vehicle out. Whether the man was crazed or not we started to do his bidding and for the second time in this last century we started to build a Burma type road. We hacked saplings down by the score; slowly and very painfully we worked the machine back towards the tarmac road, some two miles down the track. Eventually we came to a field gate that was an open bog between granite slabs - there we met our Waterloo. The Wr.L. was firmly bogged down, up to its axles in mud and animal droppings. Mr.X by now I think, was as exhausted mentally as we were physically from our woodcutting and vehicle pushing.
It was a local farmer who came to our rescue having been refused the help of his tractor initially when I asked by Jeff, suddenly became available when A.D.O.Reaney arrived to find what had happened to our appliance. With the Wr.L. freed and we eventually made it back to the road, where Reaney was waiting for us along with the workshop's recovery lorry. They had come out to give assistance, but they had decided that only a fool would have attempted to go down that track.
So they blamed Peter.

July 1973
I've finally passed both parts of the Sub Officer's examination, thanks to industrial disputes and work to rules, which gave me plenty of time to study; also Douglas for keeping me studying with him. This should mean I more or less get a Leading Fireman's job when one comes available this year. Janet rang me at work to let me know as soon as the letter of notification arrived.

Douglas told me he had passed, so it was double celebrations on the shift.

August 1973
Barry Woods has never attempted to settle down here and he makes life harder for us with his bickering. He was used to being treated like a star down on the Central station, but at an out station you all have to pull together. This man was very much admired by most of his work mates and he was given a great deal of leeway to allow him time to settle into our work routine, yet he seems to be pushing our tolerance of his idleness to the limits. This becomes more apparent when he is at a fire, for he likes to be the branch man, but doesn't like to do the running out of the hose or, come to that, the making up of it afterwards. It's our own fault, I believe, for letting him get away with so much when he first arrived, but he is pushing his luck too far when we are expected to do his duties as well as our own. Jeff and Jim have tried shaming the man into work, but all they get in response was.

"I never asked to come here, send me back as soon as you like."
Now there is nothing we would like better than for him to go back to Rocko' as we have enough to contend with in Mr.X without having a Prima Donna for a fireman. It's funny how, Down at Rocko' I didn't mind his antics, but having worked with him over a long period of time, his skiving can become a bit trying.

All would agree that when you went relieving he always made you feel welcome and I know there was a time when he personally got us out of a bollocking. It was one time when I was relieving down at Rocko'; just one minute before we were to be dismissed we had a call to an R.T.A. (Road Traffic Accident). It wasn't a serious accident, in fact it only wanted the car battery disconnecting and the road swilling free of petrol. As we stood about waiting while L.Fm. Danks collected details for his Special Service report, who should pass but Lambert, on his way to work. We all stood to attention at the edge of the road and Barry threw up a salute, which was acknowledged.

Being in the centre of town the local press were soon on the scene of the accident and several photographs were taken to appear in the following night's edition. We all had a look at the pictures and what had been written about the accident. At the time we thought nothing more about it as the article followed the usual line taken by the paper - Mr So and So aged, whatever, was involved in a motoring accident, etceteras. It was therefore a surprise that Lambert should come in early specially to interview us about the picture that accompanied the article. As we entered his office he threw the paper on the desk and enquired why we were not wearing our lamps whilst on duty, intimating that we had hung the lamps up early and technically speaking, I supposed, knocked off before time.

I would have admitted the fact, but Barry interceded by saying, "The lamps were on the belts, but you couldn't see them because they were at our backs with the lamp hung on the metal belt brackets." Lambert accepted this explanation without question, but I've a feeling a Chief doesn't get you into his office to check how you wear a lamp without being prepared to take the matter further if not satisfied.

Barry now committed a sin that we would find hard to forgive. He started to spoil our meals by either burning them or by putting in the wrong ingredients. An example of this was when the other day shift cook asked him to sprinkle some nutmeg onto the custard pie she had just finished, but Barry put on pepper instead. At Central they never had to do the actual cooking, only the serving out of meals, but at an out station you have to be both head cook and bottle washer, sometimes. Some men take to cooking like a duck takes to water, others find cooking harder, but he was the only one I've met who wasn't prepared to give it his best effort, which was all that was asked of any of us.

Jeff tried to get him to tow the line by putting him on mess duties until he got it right, but things came to a head when he left a light under the chip pan, ruining our supper and almost causing a kitchen fire. If it hadn't been for Jim going around, inspecting what Barry was doing, the kitchen would have been gutted as we had seen at many a house fire under similar circumstances.
Jeff bollocked him, but it made no difference to his attitude - he continued to be surly.

September 1973
Barry went to see Mr.X about a transfer and this led to a meeting with A.C.O. Peel who finally agreed he should be moved; not back to a station he wanted, but to Low Edges, a station even further out of his way than Elm Lane. By the middle of the month he was gone and we all breathed a sigh of relief with his departure. Although we were now under strength the news is of a vast recruiting drive taking place later this month for the opening of the new station and the re-organisation from County Borough to Metropolitan Council. With the coming of a County Council Fire Brigade there is fresh hope in many of us that we will get a promotion out of this merger. In total there are four separate County Borough Fire Brigades and one County

Division that are going to merge into what will become South Yorkshire Fire Service. A problem for someone is who will lead this new Brigade as at least three C.F.O.s think they have a strong claim to the position. For when the new boundaries have been settled it will show that the two areas contributing most land and wealth to the County will come from Sheffield and the West Ridings Brigades. So it is rumoured that Lambert will be Chief and that the Divisional Commander of three Ridings we are amalgamating with will become Deputy Chief; the other A.F.C.O.'s will keep their present rank.

Recruiting from the City has had such a large response and one wonders if they know what they are letting themselves in for. You have got to think they do, but how many are coming for the glamour - like I did - and will they be disappointed when they realise that it is a hard job that at times demands many sacrifices.

October 1973
The engine house is complete and I have queried how they are going to insert the pole into the pole chute now that the roof is more or less completed, but Mr.X said, "Just because you worked on construction you think you know it all."

Well, I shall be interested to see how they do achieve getting the pole into the chute, as for the life of me I cannot see how it will be done.
The Copper Beech tree that has stood on this site for over a hundred and forty years was today chopped down, flouting all the preservation orders that have been placed on it. I would like to know for sure if Mr.X had a hand it its demise, for by its removal the builder can now start to construct the new Breathing Apparatus Smoke House to Lambert's specifications. The local environmentalists went bananas when they discovered that the tree had been put to the axe and are seeking legal action against the Brigade.

Mr.X is under the impression that the Chief is prepared for the fine they will get, as it will cost less than having to alter the buildings to accommodate the tree when the second phase of the building work commences. It is sad that a tree, which had stood before the year 1830s and with a trunk diameter of over thirty-nine inches, should end this way.

December 1973
I am very down hearted that I haven't been given one of the many L.Fm.'s ranks that were on offer. Many, including Doug and 'Billy Bud' John Gee, had got a bar out of the first wave of promotions. Therefore I suppose it was too

much to expect that good news would abound my way now that we are to lose Mr.X to Rivelin in the coming year. Although it will be some consolation that we are to have Ken Peckett in his stead.

Events of 1973
This year has been dominated by the industrial strife once again, and the three day working week. Heath's government reels on the ropes, waiting for the final KO.

The fishing fleet are harassed by Icelandic Gun Boats so our Navy is sent to protect our fishing fleet.

Thirty died in a leisure complex fire on the Isle of Man. Roof and other building materials are said to be at fault for its rapid spread.

Petrol shortage after Israel attacks hostile Arab neighbours and wins the three-day war.

The new Elm Lane fire station

Chapter 6

Time for more changes

1974

We have had to occupy the new station living quarters as the old station has practically fallen about our ears. We lost the station heating early 1973 and the rest of the building was finally condemned when the roof started to leak. The contractors have hit several obstacles, which has postponed the handing over of the new station for several more months. One of which was that after the roof was completed and they had started to lay the engine house floor tiles, one of the workers discovered a stainless steel pole of thirty feet long and six inches in diameter. (This was the missing pole from our pole chute that I had warned them about last year.) It was decided by a group of labourers that it would easily slide into place through the engine house entrance to the chute.

I spent several happy hours watching these muscle/arse protruding trousered men, struggle to raise the pole. How they expected to bend such a large piece of metal is beyond me, but for some illogical reason they thought they could. Eventually defeat was acknowledged and a hole had to be drilled in the roof to pass the pole through.

Another setback was when they discovered that where the central appliance bay is located, so was a well that supplied the old house, dating back to 1847. Elm House was taken over at the outset of the last war and converted into a fire station in 1939, and now the new engine house floor was discovered not to be able to withstand the weight of an appliance because of the well.

All these little problems delayed the handing over, so whilst they were being resolved we used the office block and living quarters. This pleased Mr.X for he could have his last swipe at making us miserable by keeping us to a small area of the new station and making us work in the damp of the old station while he enjoyed the warmth of the new, heated offices. Thankfully we didn't have to put up with that situation for long because he left and Ken Peckett came.

Ken's coming was likened to that of a Messiah. He altered the station's attitude in one swipe; everything was to be moved into the new station and that only the appliances were to be manned from the old. Protective sheeting was rigged up to keep the worst of the weather off the waiting appliances, but we were finally going to have dry kit to wear again.

Peckett was a man in his late forties having joined the service after being demobbed from the Navy. Ken could remember me from my first days at Mansfield Rd. and I him. As then, he now appeared to be a fair dealing man - and he was. Once more our working life took on a peaceful atmosphere. A sign of his attitude came on the first day of his shift; Jeff was on leave so Jim was put in charge of the R.T. whilst he took the First Turn. Since he didn't know the area he asked if I would sit in the O.I.C. place and guide him if necessary.

The first call of the day was into Rocko's area to a house fire up on the Walkley district of the City. The roads were very icy and the light covering of snow made the climb up the steep hills difficult. In fact they were so bad that half way up the hill that the house fire we were attending, our Water Ladder started to skid and I had to bail out to put a wheel chock under its rear wheels to prevent it sliding back any further. Brian and Malc then had to go on foot up to the house wearing their B.A.'s. Whilst they were struggling up, Rocko's appliance entered the road from the top, but had the reverse of our problem for it couldn't stop coming down hill and their B.A. men had to jump out as they passed the house affected.

The occupier of the house had been refilling a paraffin heater whilst it was still lit and the excess fuel spilled around the burner, which caught fire. Realising it was a danger to the children in the house the man had tried to carry it to the outside. With flames licking around the carrying handle he made a valiant, but no less foolish effort to rid the house of the potential firebomb. Suffering the burns to his hands and arm he got to the top of the staircase that led down from his first floor flat and the entrance hall door. Madness or pain made him do the next thing, for he threw the paraffin heater down the stairs, thereby blocking off his, and the rest of the occupants' first means of escape.

When the four B.A. wearers arrived they were met with the hallway fire. From the equipment they had managed to take with them the B.A. teams extinguished the fire with a D.P. extinguisher sufficient enough for one of them to carry it outside and then, with the rest of the extinguisher contents, dowse the flame on the staircase.

The rest of us from the appliances finally managed to get Hose Reel off both appliances and by connecting it all together from our Wr.L. we got the water to them to finish off the job. Apart from our friend who had suffered burns, the rest of the multi-occupancy escaped uninjured. I was given the task of treating the man suffering from burns, so with bandages soaked in ice cool water I wrapped up his hand and lower arm before he was taken down the hill to a waiting ambulance.

From the way they were parked the appliances looked like they had been involved in an accident. Rocko's had slid sideways down the hill, nearly reaching the bottom before coming to rest in the kerb facing down hill; whilst our machine was parked obliquely to the hill.

No attempt was made by Peter to get to the top of the hill; we just tried to slide back down with more dignity than we came up. Peckett was quite pleased by our efforts at what could have been a disastrous for all concerned.

Once Rocko's personnel were able to manage we were disengaged from the fire and told to return to the station. Once again Peckett told me to sit in front and act as pathfinder if necessary. We had got onto the main road leading back to our station and were nearing Owlerton, when I witnessed a man slumped on the ground in a bus shelter. I told Peter to stop and turning to Ken I told him of what I had seen. With the first aid kit still handy I dropped off the Wr.L. and rushed back to the bus shelter. Ken ordered Malc to bring the 'Minuteman' as he and the rest followed me to the casualty. I gathered, from a woman accompanying him that he suffered from Angina. With cyanosis slowly creeping across his face I started to administer oxygen. Brian Marsden came to my side and felt for his carotid pulse. I looked across to him for his response, but he just shook his head. By this time people had started to gather around to watch the spectacle of a man fighting for his life. Unfastening his coat I removed as many restrictions as possible, then, after checking his pulse for myself, I commenced Cardiac Massage.

The man was in his early seventies and I knew I was on a sticky wicket from the outset, but you have to try. Opening his mouth I felt to make sure that his denture fitted okay, then tilting his head back I placed finger and thumb at the side of his nose and closed the airway. Covering his mouth with mine I blew into him four good puffs of air. Tracing the man's rib cage I followed it until I came to his sternum (breastbone) and then, placing two fingers over the lower cartilage of the sternum, I placed the ball of my left hand onto the sternum. Pulling back my left hand's fingers with my right hand I slowly pressed down for the first count. One - Two - Three - Four - Five - rest. The airway was inserted into his throat by Brian who then placed the oxygen mask over it and oxygen started to fill the man's lungs. With a combination of minuteman and cardiac massage we slowly saw the man's colour come back from blue to red. At first I wasn't sure if it was the minuteman pulse I could feel so for a moment we discontinued it. There was a slight pulse, which was backed up by the man gipping at the airway that he vomited out of his mouth. We kept on giving the man oxygen until the ambulance arrived and whisked his away along with his grateful, lady pensioner.

Once more we packed up our gear and prepared to make our way home. As I started to get into the front seat, Ken said, "Not bloody likely. You are a Jonah, you can get into the back; I've had enough excitement for one day."

It was good to sit up front and I reckoned I could handle what came my way, I thought. On getting back to the station we continued to prepare for the time we could let the old station go. It would have been nice to give it a Viking send off by torching it, but they wouldn't allow it - not yet any way. It is sad to see the old station steadily decay and I guess this will be the end to tramps finding somewhere warm to sleep on a winter's night, as they used to on the coke pile. There have been many a fireman who has had the shock of his life when stoking the boiler in the middle of the night, and found a foot suddenly appear from the coke bunker, attached to a cursing piece of human flotsam. A little later in the afternoon we were told that the old gentleman had died before reaching hospital. This news gutted me, as when I handed him over to the ambulance men his breathing was shallow, but by his own efforts, so why did he die? I was told this happens and I am sure it does, but I still wish I'd gone to the hospital with him to make sure that the effort we had put into saving his life was carried on until a doctor could take over.

May 1974
The new station is fully operational at last and the big pomp and ceremony will take place in August of this year. It was muted that one of the Royals has been approached to do the honours, but it is doubtful that any of the main Royal Household will attend, because of the building delays.

June 1974
My final notification came through that I had passed both parts of the Sub's examination, although I am one of the very few who haven't got a rank out of the group of men who were at Bradford with me earlier this year.

August 1974

The day has been a round of grass fires and false alarms; then D.O. Tyler came onto the station. D.O. Tyler is our new Divisional Commander and he has taken over what will be called 'East' Division, which is an amalgamation of three different brigades.

Having introduced himself to Peckett he went into his office and, behind closed doors had a long discussion with him. After about half an hour he asked to meet Jeff and Jim who went and joined Ken in the office. At one point we heard Tyler give the new Chief's opinion on Mr.X, which tallied with our own "--and I don't want this type of officer in my Division," we heard him say.

Eventually they all came out and, after the briefest of greetings to us; Tyler went on his way. Jeff watched him leave then told me to get into my undress uniform and go and see Peckett in the office.

"Sit down, Arthur, I've got to ask you one or two questions," he said.

At this point I had no idea why I was being given a second questioning on station topography and administration. About half way through Jeff joined him, but stood at the back of me and kept quiet.

"I think that's about it, Jeff, don't you?" Ken asked.

"Yup," replied Jeff, who then turned and left us alone once more.

"You've never given me any trouble and others have groused about not being made straight up to Sub, I've heard," he turned and stared out of the window, scratching his testicles as he stood. "You'll do. You start as Leading Fireman in October; on this Watch."

I was flabbergasted and happy at the same time. "Thank you, sir," I replied to the back of Ken, who was still looking out of the window.

I took it from his nonchalance that the interview had ended so I left him on his own. On seeing Jeff in the corridor, he congratulated me on being promoted and then we walked back into the mess room where the others were waiting for confirmation of what Jim had told them. It was my turn to be congratulated, but I said, "I got the impression that if there had been a turd with my qualification it would have been promoted instead of me." Yet still, I had got my first foot on the ladder and it was now up to me to see how far I could get.

Ken Peckett had been told by Tyler that he had to move house if he still wanted to be stationed here, as you have now got to live in your divisional area; this was why he looked so preoccupied after my interview. I guess it came as a shock to him, for his health started to deteriorate from then on.

September 1974
Ken Peckett has been diagnosed as suffering from depression and has started moves to take early retirement at the end of the year. On his last day on duty as Station Officer he said, "The job is changing too much for me and I don't think it's for the better. There is no way I am going to sell up my home for two pieces of chrome on each shoulder. My family comes first and always will."

Although Jeff has got the same qualifications as Richard Ash, Richard has been given the acting rank of Stn.O. Until a new one is appointed.

September 30th 1974
I am not to be Leading Fireman on Blue Watch but I am to go onto White Watch whose Sub Officer is Walt Dawes.

So came to an end my days with the rank of a Fireman and from now on I shall be an officer, albeit a junior one. I shall never forget the treatment I received as a fireman and will always treat my firemen better than I was treated at various times.

October 1974
With a kiss from Janet I set off to work this morning, a spring in my step. I had determined that as an officer I would treat the men with the respect they deserved and never forget where I came from. For a man should be true to his roots and never deny the point from whence he set off on his journey. I have seen many that changed just because they had a chrome bar on their shoulder; that, I thought, must not happen to me.

Again I was fortunate that I was starting the second part of my career with a man who also thought like I did - Walt. It had been ages since I worked with him and I hoped he would be glad I was on his shift and not think of me as 'Johnny Red'. Walt also had a keen Leading Fireman in Alan Ryder. This fair-haired smoothy was a likable man and his wife was one of those who hadn't got a fur coat, which she so much admired on other officer's wives. As the saying goes, 'behind every successful man is a woman without a fur coat.'

On arriving at work I did my first deliberate act to show the others that I had not altered by the gaining of a bar. Most officers refuse to mix with the firemen, go straight into the office and close the door behind them, thereby separating themselves from their crew and other firemen. I sat down in the mess room and I thought I would wait for Walt to welcome me onto his shift.

The evening before I had planned what type of impression I was going to make on the firemen and the officers. In the past I had seen and heard how various men, on gaining a rank, would swagger into the office as though they had always been part of the office fittings, only to achieve derision from other officers. So it was my intention that I should start off on the right footing with everybody concerned.

By 0855 hours Walt hadn't come to see where I was, nor had Alan, and I wondered if my coming onto this shift was welcomed. Even Acting Station Officer Ash hadn't sent for me, which surprised me for he had said he would formally introduce me to the shift and go over with me, his policy for running the station along with Walt. Yet there were only five minutes to go and nobody was bothering about me.

"Arth, are you coming into the office or not. You are aware that you are in charge today," enquired Varley.
I turned around and put down the morning paper I was reading.
"I thought Walt was on," I replied.
"No. Ash's gone off sick and Walt and Alan are on leave, so you, my old son, have got it all," smiled Tom.

Well, there is no better time to learn how to swim as than when you are in the deep end of the swimming pool. All my plans were falling apart around me. I'd been led to expect that I would be eased gently into my rank and new position on the shift, yet here I was, on my own, in charge of 32 square miles of fire risk, two fire engines and seven firemen. Tom told me what projects were outstanding and the equipment that needed urgent attention.
"Any problems, give me a ring," he added at the end of his hand-over talk.
With that he donned his cap and opened the office door to allow me to take my first parade and roll call.

"Parade, SHUN!" I snapped out.
The two crews snapped to attention.
"Carry on, off going Watch," I said to Tom
"Red Watch, DISMISSED."
With that, the night shift took a half turn to the right and fell out to make their way home.
I stood looking down the line of faces and they in turn were eyeing me up to see what I was about to inflict upon them. Although I knew all of them as firemen we were strangers to one another as officer and crew. My next choice of words would seal my fate for the day.

"Good morning, Gentlemen," I began.

I had heard those words spoken by the weather forecaster for shipping on the Light Programme of the BBC radio for years before I set off for the steel works, and when he was asked one time why he began each morning broadcast with those words he said:

"The men I am addressing are far out at sea, risking their lives to make a living and they deserve some respect."

I believed the men assembled in front of me deserved just as much respect.

"My name is Arthur Levick and I am your new Leading Fireman," I formally introduced myself. "Now please answer the roll call."

"Fireman Briddon."

"Here."

"Fireman Jones."

"Here."

"Fireman Egan."

"Here."

I went down the list on the manning board, and then asked, "Who is next in line for acting up rank to be the O.I.C. of the H.P."

"Dunno, I think it's either me or Egan," replied Vin Briddon.

"Right, Vin, you take the H.P. and Fireman Jones can be your driver."

One problem down, only another million to sort out, I thought. I continued to detail the day's duties to the rest of the crew and finally I said, "After the appliance checks have been completed I want you all dressed for drill in your fire-kit, but to muster in the mess room. This is to give us all a chance to get to know one another. White Watch, SHUN! Checking duties - FALL OUT!"

"Vin, who is the mess man?" I enquired.

"I am."

"Right, I'd like to have a brew of tea for us all whilst I talk." Not knowing how they went on for paying for extra mashing, I offered to pay.

"No, we can afford a cuppa," said Vin as he went to start the checking off of the H.P. with Stan.

I returned to the office and got out the attendance register and marked off the appropriate columns. The only bit of farsightedness that I'd done was to make out an idiot book of the daily running of a station, in the days after I had been told I was to be promoted; I was now frantically reading this book.

A knock came on the office door and in walked Vin. "Tea's mashed," he smiled. "Bet tha didn't expect to be thrown in the deep end straight away!"

"No, I must admit I didn't, but we will manage," I said, reassuring myself more than him. In the mess room I gave my first introductory speech based on the others I'd heard from visiting officers, then I took them out for drill keeping it to a plain, basic ladder and pump exercise. The men were competent, as I would have expected of any of Walt's crews, which pleased me. At least, no matter what today brought before me, I knew I had a good crew. The early part of the morning quickly passed by and once more we were sat down to another tea break, but this time it was official; also this time it was me who was being cross examined as to what I did, what I liked and more to the point - how much I was going to go by the brigade orders. I told them my policy would depend on what Walt wanted to achieve and since I hadn't had a chance to speak to anybody today I would be playing it by ear.

After finishing my cup of tea I went back into the office to consult my idiot book for my next move. It was whilst reading this book I got the thing I had hoped for most, but dreaded with equal trepidation - my first Fire call.

I listened as the Tannoy blurted out the address, writing it down on the palm of my hand with a chinagraph pencil.

77 Henry Street

Grimesthorpe

Map Reference

Lima 1, 2, Mike 1

Appliances

Water Ladder Echo 5

Chimney Fire.

I moved quickly from the office and ran down the corridor to the engine house. Climbing into the front seat of the appliance I started to get dressed in my fire-kit. Dave Egan checked about him and then looked across to me.

"Let's go!" I said.

The engine roared as he set off and I reached for the radio handset down in front of me.

"Echo 5, mobile. 77 Henry Street. Leading Fireman Levick - O.I.C.," I replaced the receiver back into its housing and continued to get dressed.

I went through the procedures of dealing with a chimney fire in my mind and for the first time realised how lonely it was to sit up in the front seat, although I was thankful my first fire was nothing but a simple bread and butter issue. The men didn't need any instructions, although I gave them, for just like me they knew what was required and did it out of routine. As I supervised the extinguishing of the fire and the safety checks afterwards the men were assessing me to see if I was a flapper, flannelling, or just a plain incompetent officer. As I entered the details of the fire into my virgin notebook I had a look around and I think we had all come through the first test with a pass grade at least.

My calls hadn't finished for the day with that one, for by the time 1800 hours had arrived I had received one S.S. call, an F.A. call to the Hospital and a small house fire, which only required checking as the occupier had extinguished it before our arrival. In between firefighting I had attended to some of the problems, left by Tom, and the others were put into abeyance or were passed onto the new night shift and Sub Officer Overton.

When I got home Janet wanted to know how I had faired and so I went over the days events that I'm sure bored her to death, but she listened anyway. She in turn told me of her day and that was equally as boring; however, one thing she mentioned was that she wouldn't mind going back to work again as soon as possible. For even though I'd had a pay rise from my promotion and we could look forward to my annual pay rise as well, the political climate made household budgeting very difficult. What with strikes and inflation she thought our money would soon be eaten away and that she could give us that buffer others had enjoyed for so long.

We had noticed the only people who didn't complain about the cost of things were those whose wives were earning and when you said you found it hard to manage they would reply.

"It's how you manage your money."
Although when pressed about how much they had coming into their homes to compare with yours you quickly discovered these financial wizards not only had a wife's wage as an extra income, but a part time wage of their own as well.

Senior officers were the worst for this self-righteous attitude of telling you how to live, but also we had their new tedious discussion to listen to as well - their holiday abroad.

Nothing can be of less interest to another, than how you spent a week, ten days or a fortnight baking in the sun. Of how you discovered this tiny hosteria that served traditional Spanish food used only by the locals and four million German tourists. Along with how travel had broadened their minds to such an extent that they were going completely native and having a patio attached to their house. So they could watch the English summer rain fall on coloured slabs of concrete instead of their muddy garden with its genuine garden fountain straight from Woolworths.

The next day Walt was back and he said he was sorry I had been left on my own.

"I preferred it that way," I said. "I have now got my first fires under my belt and out of the way; unlike some who have to go through that experience of how they will manage when it's their time to sit up in front."
"Very true, I had the same thing happen to me when I got made up. Fireman one day, Officer the next," said Walt

Over the coming weeks I settled into becoming part of Walt's team. He treats everybody equally and I, as the junior rank, was given equal status from the beginning. Which pleased me for I thought I would have been treated like the hand rag, since Alan had nearly twelve months' seniority to me as a L.Fm. - but I had three years more service in than him to compensate.
It was agreed with Alan that we should man on alternate days the special (H.P.), since the R.T. had been exchanged for it and, and do the other as B.A. wearer in the back of the Water Ladder. This arrangement was thought to be a good one for it made our working relationship excellent, as there was no jealousy of favouritism.

December 1974
I was on the H.P. Although I couldn't drive I still had qualified as a cage operator, which was just as important, for as O.I.C. you had a greater input as to how the cage was to be used. Today my driver was Steve Blanchard who, although still in his probation period, was passed out as a driver since he held a Class One driving licence. This man had a head on his shoulders that greatly maligned his age. Right from my first journey with him I knew he was in full control and not like some of our drivers, who get what used to be called 'bell happy'. This affection used to make the quietest of men drive like the devil. They drove not just fast, but dangerously and when sat at the side of such a man you felt that your insurance cover was never sufficient. Briddon was such a man who became 'bell happy' when responding to a call and I'd already given him a warning to slow down when responding to one call, but he told me to 'stop whittling'.

We had drilled all morning with the H.P. on the station, but Walt was seeking permission to go down to the local derelict buildings and do additional training on site. The hierarchy seemed to agree with this type of training, especially since the first batch of recruits that have completed their course have come back onto station not knowing how to use the Ajax ladder, which still is a major piece of equipment on this brigade.

We have been told that a large shake up of personnel will take place, although no one will be moved off their present station. This is to try and balance up the various shifts, for some have a service average of ten years and others now have a service average of less than four. The new Divisional Commander, apart from being a stickler for radio communications corresponding to the drill book, doesn't seem to realise that this imbalance of service is a problem that is waiting to explode in his - or our - faces. No matter how good the training school it cannot replace actual firefighting experience and, at this present time, fire crews with experience are thin on the ground. Walt has voiced his opinions as well as Richard on this matter, but they don't seem to heed the warnings that are being given to them.

Sheffield and Rotherham are two big, heavy industrial steel producers and the experienced men that were teethed on the risks thrown up by this type of industry have been scattered about with the vast amounts of promotion. Those that have been sent to replace them are only book wise to the risks and book knowledge plus inexperienced firemen has got to lead to a disaster.

Once more I put my foot into my mouth when the new Divisional Commander made a flying visit to meet his fire crews. These visits have been undertaken in his off duty time, for as he has said, "The new brigade will take years to actually jell as one organisation and I am as aware as the next man that the amalgamation has produced rivalry amongst the different brigades now having to work as one."

Around this point his mouth started to dry up and, having suffered at various times with this type of nervous condition, I asked, "Seeing that it is near to our tea break, could a cup of tea be mashed and we can listen to your talk as we drink." I had hoped that he would realise that I had only done this so he could talk in a relaxed atmosphere, because the man's presence and bearing are very oppressive to say the least.

Vin mashed the tea and I gave D.O. Dennis Tyler the first cup, passing round the others. Tyler looked at the cup and then back to me.
"Do you always serve tea in cups without a saucer," he asked.
"Yes, we progressed years ago from supping out of the saucers," I replied jokingly.

"Don't be facetious, Leading Fireman," he snapped back.
Oh my God! Another one, who will want a separate officer's club in the near future, I thought. After he gave us our pep talk and I accompanied him back

to the office, along with Walt, it didn't take him long to bring up the matter of saucers and my remarks afterwards. He laid into my attitude good and proper, saying he would overlook the matter this time, but on future occasions I was to show him the respect of his rank. I tried to give my side of the story but he wouldn't hear any of it. After he had gone Walt said that if he wants to go by the book it would suit him fine.

Walt's attitude was, if you kept to the strict regulations you couldn't go far wrong, and with men like this in charge it would be the only way to proceed if you wanted an easy life. Over the last few months since my promotion I had come to realise that the L.Fm. was in a cast between the Devil and the deep blue sea. You were no longer a fireman and they were always suspicious of your motives, but you were not high enough in rank to have any clout of the other ranks. They say it's tough at the top, but by gum it's harder at the bottom.

The year ended with a night out with the shift and their wives. Janet said that in future she would not attend as she felt she had so little in common with any of them.

Janet was a plain and simple woman who liked to call a spade a spade and the airs and graces that abounded that night were not to her liking. She, like me, is fed up of tales of summer holidays and how well their children are progressing at school. The night would have been a complete washout for her if she hadn't met up with Jim and his wife Vera who were out celebrating their wedding anniversary.

Another mixed Christmas of holiday and work. After nearly eleven years I have had only one complete festive period off. I should like to be able to join in the fun without having to excuse myself, part way through, to slope off to work.

Events of 1974

This year has been a real mixture of events, from my promotion to Keith starting up in business. The last two elections saw Labour gain power by a tiny majority, but the last one in October saw them increase their seat in Parliament by 3 over the rest of the political parties. The miners got a fantastic pay rise and later on in the year the new social wage's contract was agreed with the T.U.C. - as usual we are losers in the pay rounds.

Princess Anne suffered an attempted kidnapping whilst driving down The Mall; her husband, Mark Phillips, is said to have saved her.

The largest fire seen for many months occurred at Flixborough and several pumps went from South Yorkshire. Twenty-nine people were killed in the blast and fire that followed.

Lord Lucan has vanished after being accused of killing the family's nanny, Sandra Rivett.

One missing, one found; John Stonehouse went missing after doing a Reginald Perrin, (a TV character who tried to fake suicide), on a Miami Beach. He was later discovered in Australia with his secretary, Sheila Buckley. Stonehouse is involved with money missing from the Bangladeshi Bank of which he was the Chairman.

Postscript

During the course of this book some names have been protected to save embarrassment. Although all the stories are true as to my recollection and notes from diaries and incident notes

Reference Terminology

Rank

Fm.	Fireman
L.Fm.	Leading Fireman
Sub O.	Sub Officer
Stn.O.	Station Officer
A.D.O.	Assistant Divisional Officer
D.O.	Divisional Officer
A.C.F.O.	Assistant Chief Fire Officer
C.F.O.	Chief Fire Officer

Appliances

Wr.T	Water Tender
P.E.	Pump Escape
R.T.	Rescue Tender
T.T.L.	Turntable Ladder
Wr. C.	Wireless Car

Ajax Ladder	35 foot extension Ladder
Rounds	Rungs of a ladder

Horns	Top space between last round and strings.
Strings	Side members of a ladder
Hook Ladder	Single section ladder 13.5 feet long. With a retractable hook when not in use. This hook 2.33 feet long with its six inch Bill. Was used in the past by Firemen to gain access to high building where 45 foot Escape ladder couldn't reach. By the 1960s it was mainly used to give recruits confidence with ladder climbing co-ordination and height working.

Hose	Canvas or Rubber lined Flexible tube for conveying liquids.
Branch	A Hose fitting of metal or combination of both plastic and metal parts terminating with a nozzle.
Nozzle	Converts water pressure energy into velocity or kinetic Energy.
B.A.	Breathing Apparatus.